THE GLORIOUS STRUGGLE

How the United States Became a Nation

BOOKS BY BURT HIRSCHFELD

THE
GLORIOUS
STRUGGLE

How the United States
Became a Nation

by BURT HIRSCHFELD

HAWTHORN BOOKS, INC.—Publishers—New York

1

It was the "starving time" in the New World.

The winter of 1610 lay harsh and unrelenting on the peninsula alongside the James River in Virginia. Here was situated the colony of Jamestown, established by the men of the London Company under charter of King James, their aim to spread the Christian religion among "the Infidels and Savages," and to return economic gain to the shareholders.

Jamestown was to be England's foothold in America, the beginnings of empire, a territory settled by her many unemployed, who would then grow productive and contribute to the good of the kingdom, swelling its coffers and increasing its glory.

Hope was high in the breasts of the 144 men and boys who had set out from London on December 20, 1606, commissioned to "spy out the land," secure in the ships *Sarah Constant, Goodspeed,* and *Discovery,* under the command of Captain Christopher Newport. But the North Atlantic treated them cruelly, and when the small fleet put into Chesapeake Bay in April only 104 men were still alive.

The two capes at the entrance to the bay were named Charles and Henry, in honor of the royal family, and a thrust of land was called Point Comfort. Grateful to be alive and ashore, the men decided that this Virginia was a likely place to settle.

One of them, George Percy, described the region in glowing terms: "Flowers of divers kinds and colours . . . the goodly trees . . . as Cedars, Cipresse and other Kinds . . . fine and beautiful Strawberries, foure times bigger and better than ours in England . . . Squirrels, Conies, Black Birds with crimson wings, and divers other Fowles and Birds of divers and sundry Collours . . ."

But those "Knights, Gentlemen, Merchants, and other Adventurers" were poorly suited for the rigors of life in Virginia. Few of them possessed either the skills needed to survive in the wilderness, the will to acquire them, or a willingness to work hard. Trouble erupted early, many of the men refusing to labor for the collective good.

"It's my own fortune I'm here to find," said one, "and not to raise callouses on my hands."

Agreement was general. "Adventure is why we came, adventure, gold, and glory, and a swift return to England."

"There'll be none of that for any of us," Captain John Smith insisted, angered by this indolence and selfishness. "There are wild savages in the forest, and unless we plant and build we'll suffer from them and from the adverse elements."

His warnings went unheeded. Even his colleagues on the ruling council could not agree on what to do to improve the situation.

"The gentlemen of the company," said Edward Maria Wingfield, "must be permitted to act in a manner as will profit themselves and the shareholders and it is not our purpose to instruct them in the manner proper to accomplish that end."

"Without a suitable amount of work there can only be disaster," Smith insisted.

Wingfield rejected the captain's point of view. "The Spanish to the south have plucked gold off the ground and from the natives. Our people may well do likewise."

"The Spaniards are of no concern in this place," Smith responded. "The difficulties that exist in Virginia must be faced by us, the problems solved."

Smith's arguments did little good. The members of the company tended to side with Wingfield and could not be moved to act in their own behalf. Poorly fed and clothed, many men fell victim to disease, and a number of them died. Winter was the worst time, extracting a heavy toll in human life. One cold January day, a terrifying cry was raised.

"Fire!"

No one knew how it had started, but the flames raged through the tiny settlement, destroying most of the buildings. Then a freshet of wind turned the blaze, and it was John Smith who first recognized the new danger.

"The corn!" he cried. "Protect the corn supply."

The small building which housed the grain was vulnerable, and its burning would destroy their entire winter's supply. The men came running with axes and spades. Digging trenches around the storehouse, chopping down nearby trees, they created a firebreak. At last it was done, the fire extinguished, the corn saved.

But the desperate effort had been for nothing. Later that winter, hungry rats burrowed into the storehouse and devoured almost all the corn.

For the men of Jamestown, the focus of struggle was crystallized—to survive. Many lost the fight, and, of those who lived, a majority were too weak and sick to help themselves. Nature itself seemed to conspire against them: the James River was icy and forbidding, the forest was a great green trap alive with wild beasts and hostile Indians, the nearby swamp a source of illness and death.

The future of the settlement grew dim, survival depending on the arrival of supplies from England, supplies which never came. Tempers grew short and frictions increased.

"Let's leave this terrible place," Wingfield said.

"Yes," others echoed. "We should return to England and safety."

"Not until we've fulfilled our purpose," John Smith insisted. "We came to make a colony and it still can be done."

Differences drove the men further apart, and changes were made. In the weeks that followed, first one then another president of the governing council were deposed and two members removed. One was shot for mutiny. Not even that drastic action unified the company, and all discipline seemed about to evaporate. A strong hand was needed and it was John Smith who supplied it.

Despite opposition, he managed to assume the presidency of the colony. Once in power, he established himself as a virtual dictator, issuing orders arbitrarily, ruling with an iron fist. He sent the men into the woods to chop down trees and

Captain John Smith.

make logs for a blockhouse to serve as a fortress. Untrained and unused muscles ached and soft hands rebelled. One man finally heaved his axe aside and with a string of oaths vowed to do no more work.

John Smith retrieved the tool and handed it back to him. "Blaspheme once more," he said grimly, "and you'll suffer just punishment, a quantity of cold water poured down your sleeve."

No one doubted Smith's ability to inflict such punishment, and complaints were heard less frequently after that, though there was no lessening of discontent. Smith was a harsh and demanding leader. He insisted that a well be dug, twenty houses of mud and wattle built, and bricks made for a church. Every man was expected to do his share. There was to be no further hunting for gold. Livestock and chickens were to be raised and forty acres of corn planted, thus providing for the future.

Smith's best efforts were not enough. Even the arrival of several hundred new settlers didn't help, and once again the elements took their measure until only fifty men still lived. The colonists became increasingly rebellious; and in London the shareholders began to complain about the lack of profits. Something had to be done.

A new charter was issued with control of the company passing from the King to the shareholders. Thomas West, Lord De la Warr (Delaware) was named "governor and captain general." Nine ships were outfitted to relieve Jamestown, and Sir Thomas Gates was appointed as interim governor for Lord De la Warr. The expedition sailed amid great fervor and optimism, only to run into rough seas and powerful storms which drove the ships off course. They were wrecked on the Bermuda Islands, which were claimed for England.

When Sir Thomas Gates finally arrived at Jamestown, he found the men starving, reduced to eating roots and snakes, many of them out of their minds. Convinced the situation was hopeless, he loaded the men aboard ship and set sail for England. He made it only to the mouth of the James River, where he was met by Lord De la Warr arriving with three ships, one hundred-fifty men, and supplies in abundance. They put back to shore to make another effort.

Jamestown survived, the first of the English colonies along the eastern seaboard of North America, the uncertain beginning of what would one day become the United States.

Snow was already falling over New England when the *Mayflower* dropped anchor off Cape Cod in November 1620. Aboard were fifty men, eighteen women, and thirty-four children, come to the New World out of conscience, seeking the right to worship as they pleased. Called Saints, or Puritans, they were in revolt against the ecclesiastical supremacy of the English King. Dissenting from the canons of the Church of England (the Anglican Church), they denounced it as "a halfway house between a corrupt and a pure church."

Not all the passengers aboard the *Mayflower* were Saints.

Some were called Strangers, members of the Anglican Church, but having no quarrel with it. The Strangers were not after spiritual salvation. They sought a free land and a chance to improve their material well-being and social status. The Strangers were not concerned with the religious practices of the Saints, but the latter felt otherwise.

"These Strangers," some of the Saints pointed out warily, "present an affront to Almighty God with their shameful rituals. We have departed England on a long and perilous journey in order to be rid of the Church of England and we find it aboard this vessel with us. We must be protected from the Anglican Church and its evil doctrines."

A decision was reached among the leaders of the company: the Anglican service would henceforth be prohibited aboard the *Mayflower*.

"By what right," the Strangers demanded, "do you forbid us to worship the Almighty in our own way?"

The protest fell on deaf and righteous ears. The irony of a people seeking religious freedom denying it to others went unmarked by the Saints.

All the Pilgrims overlooked other things as well. When at last they put into harbor in the New World not far from what would one day become Plymouth, Massachusetts, they discovered they were in the wrong place.

Their grant directed them to Virginia, but they were too far north. Not only did they lack title to this land, but they possessed no body of law by which to exist, no basis for orderly government.

Afraid that chaos would result, they decided to take preventive measures. A meeting was called. Forty-one of the adult males gathered in the ship's cabin and by the flickering light of a fish-oil lamp drew up what came to be known as the Mayflower Compact:

In the name of God, Amen. We, whose names are underwritten . . . having undertaken . . . a voyage to plant the first colony in the northern parts of Virginia, do . . . combine ourselves together into a civil body politic . . . and by virtue hereof to enact, constitute, and frame such just and equal laws, ordinances, acts, constitutions, and offices, from time to time, as shall be thought most meet and convenient for the general good of the colony, unto which we promise all due submission and obedience.

By this independent act the Pilgrims created their own commonwealth, subsequently choosing John Carver as governor, perhaps the first time such a post was filled by the votes of those to be governed.

Plymouth and Jamestown were the beginnings. Other colonies followed. Several communities came into being along Massachusetts Bay. A fishing post at Cape Ann failed, and some of those settlers moved south to found the town of Salem. They dispatched word back to England that here would be a haven for the religiously persecuted.

In 1628, the New England Company was chartered and a year afterward re-chartered as the Massachusetts Bay Company. No English council governed this company, control being entirely in the hands of the settlers. Massachusetts Bay was made up not only of working men, but of men of means as well, who possessed qualities of leadership so important to a new colony.

Offshoots of Massachusetts were New Hampshire and Maine. But the combination of little sponsor interest and the tendency on the part of the settlers to look to Massachusetts for guidance and help made their progress slow.

Religious bigotry and intolerance was rampant in Massachusetts, and banishment, or worse, was the punishment for those heretics who failed to conform to life in "a city of God on earth . . ."

Such a man was Roger Williams, son of a merchant-tailor, graduate of Cambridge University, and Puritan theologian. Though new to Boston in 1631, Williams soon made a reputation as a persistent critic of the Puritan Church.

"The clergy," he announced, "are false hirelings. They preach a false doctrine and have permitted their churches to become ulcered and gangrened. They must be doctored and brought back to spiritual health."

Friends sought to warn Williams that he was exposing himself to a very real danger. "The heads of the Church will not allow you to criticize them with immunity. They exercize secular as well as ecclesiastical authority and power."

"I will not be silenced," he replied. "You express the heart of my argument. No civil government owns the right to say go to this or that Church or be punished. More, religious intolerance is an insidious practice."

"Can a single man change the way matters are?"

"One man must try. Indeed, matters have to be altered. Religious errors must be corrected with religious weapons. Offenses to God are matters for a man's own conscience, not the province of any magistrate. Even more, I deny the right of King or company to grant title to the land on this continent. It belongs by every right to the Indians who inhabited this place before us."

Here was a statement that alarmed the leaders of the Massachusetts Bay Colony, far more than Williams' lack of religious orthodoxy. The colonial charter was considered a weak document on which to make a legal stand, and they wanted no public discussion launched.

A meeting of church leaders took place and a decision was reached. "The ends of the colony would be more profitably served without this Roger Williams."

"How are we to get rid of him?"

"Do we possess the authority to punish him for his words and his acts?"

"Perhaps not. But in England he could be properly dealt with."

"Exactly. In London he could be tried for treason and executed. At the least, he would have both his ears lopped off."

Williams preferred exile. With five friends, he fled into the wilderness and made it through a severe winter, later finding safety among the Narragansett Indians. From them Williams purchased land on which he built the town of Providence, in 1636, the start of what would become Rhode Island.

Here he was joined by others who felt as he did. A plantation covenant was written which included most of Williams' philosophies, incorporating the people into a fellowship, but "only in civil things." The radical concept of separation of church and state was established. Rhode Island was the first government in Christendom actually to put into effect the principle of religious freedom.

Elsewhere along the eastern shore, other Englishmen sought to build new lives for themselves. The Connecticut River Valley was a strategic military area and a vital route for fur traders. Here the land was rich and fertile, more suited to agriculture than was any other sector of New England.

In 1636, Reverend Thomas Hooker led about a hundred people into the valley, settling on the site of Hartford. Hooker made the move for political as well as religious motives, objecting to the limitations of suffrage in the Massachusetts Bay Colony. Hooker put forth an idea considered by many to be revolutionary: ". . . the foundation of authority is laide in the consent of the governed . . . the choice of the magistrate belongs to the people . . . those which have power to appoint officers, have also the right to set bounds to their authority."

In 1643, the Confederation of New England came into being, a union of settlements for mutual protection. Four colonies were involved: Massachusetts, Plymouth, Connecticut, and New Haven. All had similar problems, similar interests. They were threatened by Indians on all borders, by the Dutch to the west, and the French to the north; and, with the outbreak of civil war in England in 1642, no substantial aid could be expected from that source.

Other English colonies were created in different ways and were managed differently also. Maryland was chartered to George Calvert, Lord Baltimore, in 1632. On his death, his older son, Cecilius, became the proprietor of a ten-million-acre estate, an almost private preserve.

In 1663, a large portion of the Atlantic coast was turned over to eight favored courtiers of Charles II—it was Carolina. Profit was the primary aim of the promoters, though formation of the colony was also a blow at Spain, then firmly ensconced in Florida; in addition, this stretched the Anglo-French frontier along the southern Mississippi Valley.

Further north, a Dutch colony, New Netherland, reached from the Connecticut River to the Delaware River, including Long Island. England coveted this territory with its superb harbor, its great river leading into the Mohawk Valley. Charles II took direct action; he dispatched a fleet of four warships to New Amsterdam, the village on Manhattan Island. Terms of surrender were offered and promptly rejected by the iron-fisted governor, Peter Stuyvesant. But in the end he gave in, for his people had little will to resist. New Amsterdam fell almost without firing a shot, and with it all of New Netherland. England now had control of the military and economic center of the continent, closing the gap between the Chesapeake and the New England colonies. The new acquisition was renamed New York, in honor of the Duke of York. New Jersey was the next colony to be established, and then Pennsylvania.

The last English colony in America was Georgia. With Spain edging northward from Florida, it was decided to place another barrier in her way. The result was a charter to James Oglethorpe in 1732. Georgia was paternalistic in form, populated mainly with Englishmen who hoped to avoid debtor's prison.

The thirteen colonies thrived. Their populations expanded. These were independent men who claimed the "rights of Englishmen" no matter how far they were from home, or how often officials forgot to honor that citizenship. More and more they acted on their own authority as circumstances conditioned them to look after their own welfare. They chipped away at the institutions of the Crown, a subtle but constant struggle for supremacy. With each reluctantly conceded slice of freedom, the colonists acted in a more independent fashion.

Soon colonists were seeking more land for themselves in areas where they could profit and live unhindered while they raised their families. They moved west.

England made no effort to halt the westward flow of her

View of old New Amsterdam, now New York.

colonists; the more, and deeper, roots they put down, the more they strengthened the Empire against her enemies, Spain and France. Spain had gotten quickly into the colonial race in America, but her treasures were being drained away by European wars. She was slipping fast as a major power, and England was anxious to speed the process; the two nations went to war with each other eight times in a little over a hundred years.

It was France who troubled the westering colonists. France, firmly situated in Canada, allied with many Indian nations, thrust of her power deep into the continent along the Great Lakes and into the Mississippi Valley. This was an empire based on the fur trade, so great unpopulated stretches remained between outposts. Unable to settle the country as the English were doing, France did the next best thing—she limited the expansion of her enemy. The French erected a circle of forts from Niagara to Fort Toulouse, on the Alabama River. But the English kept coming.

The Hudson's Bay Company established posts in areas the French considered their own. An English fort at Halifax balanced French power at Louisbourg, and English land speculators and traders encouraged people to move into the Ohio Valley. A road was laid to encourage trade and migration.

The French took a dim view of all this, and built a string of fortifications around Lake Erie and on the Allegheny River. This alarmed the English. Robert Dinwiddie, governor of Virginia, a member of the Ohio Company, and a land speculator in his own right, decided to warn the French against further encroachment. He cast about for a "Person of Distinction" to head the mission, and came up with a twenty-one-year-old surveyor from a prominent family— George Washington.

Washington led a small party into the wilderness. He made several contacts with the Indians, talked with the French agent, and visited some of the forts. Ending up at Le Boeuf, he met with Commandant St. Pierre and warned him that "the lands upon the River Ohio . . . are so notoriously known to be the property of the Crown of Great Britain that it is a matter of equal concern and surprise . . . to her that a body of French forces are erecting fortresses . . ."

St. Pierre dismissed Washington's protests: ". . . as to the summons . . . to retire, I do not think myself obliged to obey it."

Diplomatic attempts to resolve the areas of dispute failed and preparations for war were made. At the same time, twenty-three delegates from the English colonies, headed by Benjamin Franklin of Pennsylvania, gathered at Albany in order to insure the friendship of the Six Nations (Iroquois Indians) and provide for their mutual interests and protection.

Franklin, already established as a publisher, tradesman, natural philosopher with a widening reputation, and a man of broad tastes active in the affairs of the land, offered a solution which became known as the Albany Plan of Union. But he was not optimistic about its chances for acceptance:

All the Assemblies in the Colonies have, I suppose, had the Union Plan laid before them, but it is not likely, in my Opinion that any of them will act upon it so far as to agree to it, or to propose any Amendments to it. Everyone cries, a union is absolutely necessary, but when they come to a Manner and Form of the union, their weak Noddles are perfectly distracted.

He was right. The Albany Plan was rejected by the colonies. But the idea had been born. The need for colonial union was clear, and it would simmer in American minds until the time for it came into being.

England was compelled to do something about the worsening military situation in the colonies, less to protect the colonists than her own interests. General Edward Braddock was ordered to the New World. At the head of 1,400 regular troops, plus 450 colonials under Lieutenant Colonel George Washington, he plunged into the forest. His goal: to capture Fort Duquesne.

Nothing went right for Braddock. Illness and the rigors of life in the field took its toll of the redcoats; expected Indian reinforcements never materialized. In order to transport heavy cannon, the soldiers carved a road through the woods, a remarkable but self-defeating operation.

At last the exhausted troops reached the Monongahela River, about eight miles from Fort Duquesne. Here they came under French and Indian attack, suffering heavy losses. Braddock himself was mortally wounded, and it was Washington who led the survivors back to Fort Cumberland.

"We have been beaten," he said, "most shamefully beaten, by a handful of Men."

The English suffered other defeats, at Fort Niagara, at Fort William Henry, in central New York, and in Europe itself. In the Old World this conflict was called the Seven Years War, while the fighting in America was called the French and Indian War. Only in the beginning, however, did matters go badly for the English. William Pitt, principal Secretary of State, instituted reforms, replacing incompetent

Lieutenant Colonel George Washington in charge of forest battle during the French and Indian War.

officers with young and skillful soldiers. Even more important, he supplied large amounts of money to Frederick of Prussia, England's ally, thus keeping France occupied in Europe. Frederick's military brilliance was such that Pitt later commented: "America was conquered in Germany."

With the fall of Quebec, England triumphed in North America. She took over France's possessions in Canada, and everything east of the Mississippi River. except the Isle of Orleans.

Some Englishmen claimed that the acquisition of Canada was a serious mistake. William Burke expressed it this way: ". . . if the people of our colonies find no check from Canada, they will extend themselves almost without bounds in the inland parts."

Others felt differently, viewing Canada as a vast marketplace that promised huge profits. A group of English merchants stated their attitude in blunt terms:

> The British Colonies are to be regarded . . . as subservient to the commerce of their mother country; the Colonies are merely factors for the purpose of trade, and in all considerations concerning the Colonies, this must always be the leading idea.

This was the view that prevailed. And so the future of the thirteen separate and already obstreperous colonies was sealed. Britain was now the most powerful nation in the world, and no European country could limit her ambitions. Her highly situated citizens, concerned with their own interests and profits, failed to perceive the changes taking place in the New World, failed to heed the mutterings of discontent, failed to understand the nature of the colonists, and so moved inexorably toward a confrontation that would shake the Empire and change the entire world.

3

Peace brought with it two results bound to maneuver England and her American colonies into conflict. England's new status as the world's foremost imperial power was the first, and the colonies' burgeoning sense of their own apartness, their Americanism, was the other.

With the threat of the French and the Spanish removed, only the Indians remained to oppose the ambitions of the settlers. And there was an increasing urgency to act independently of the motherland. All restrictions from London were resented intensely.

There were the Navigation Acts, for example, which

dictated shipping and trade policies in keeping with an economic theory called mercantilism, designed to bring as much profit as possible to England. Under these acts many colonial products—sugar, indigo, tobacco, cotton—had to be shipped to England before they could be sold.

In seeking to limit the commercial activities of the colonies, England drove a wedge between herself and the colonists, making them rely more upon themselves in a variety of matters. They became increasingly aware of their own importance, and there was much that drew them together.

For the most part, they were Englishmen, with a common heritage, and mainly of the Protestant faith. The exception: were the Scotch-Irish and Germans, and the growing number of slaves, who provided a large proportion of the manpower while reaping few of the rewards.

The English settlers were the driving force and the glue. Being, in the main, men of the soil, their attitudes and needs were similar no matter where they lived. There was widespread individual ownership of property, which resulted in a narrowing of the gap between rich and poor. A man might not be as wealthy as his neighbor, but he had his house, his land, and a productive way of life.

But the Navigation Acts, and the Molasses Act of 1733, angered the colonists.

"By what right does the King demand sixpence on each gallon of molasses brought into the colonies?" New Englanders asked each other.

"The duty is placed only on that molasses which comes from sources outside the Empire," staunch loyalists pointed out.

"Indeed, to the profit of the sugar plantations of the West Indies," Boston merchants and shippers complained.

"To pay such a tax will sooner or later cripple the rum business in New England."

"It is the law," the loyalists ended smugly.

"Making a law is one thing," a veteran merchant ship captain said quietly. "Enforcing it still another."

His listeners were anxious to hear more and urged him to continue.

The captain said: "I know customs officers and port captains all along the coast, good Englishmen all, who never turn palms down to a coin, men most agreeable to do business with."

That drew a favorable response; one man alone objected. "Pay the bribe and a man may as well pay the tax. Either is profit out of his pocket. There are other ways."

"And those are?"

"It's easy enough to take a cargo of rum into the creeks of Narragansett Bay or into Long Island Sound and put it ashore out of sight of any King's agents. Let them whistle for their sixpence."

He was not alone. Smuggling was an accepted activity along the seaboard, and any captain apprehended and brought to trial had little to fear from a jury of his peers. Matters proceeded without conflict for a while, the new duties causing no hardship.

Then England's outlook changed. She had become the prime imperial nation in the world. That meant it was vital to create and maintain a powerful political empire. To accomplish this, controls had to be tightened and colonial administrations shored up. These reforms cost money, and Parliament took steps to raise funds, thereby embarking on a collision course with the colonists.

The customs service was reorganized and the acts of trade enforced. Plans were made to raise money to pay for the troops stationed in the colonies, money to pay the salaries of the royal governors and other officials. It fell upon a new monarch to oversee this policy.

George III was the wrong man for the job, unequipped by nature and temperament. Only twenty-two when he ascended the throne, he owned no personal distinction and was in fact appallingly ignorant. He was eleven before he learned to read and never mastered spelling or punctuation or grammar. Gripped by a pervading sense of his own inadequacy, hopeless about the future, he was without vitality and had no zest for life. Though he understood little about the world he was supposed to govern, George III felt the weight of the empire upon his narrow shoulders and always to remind him there was the echo of his mother's repeated admonition:

"George," she would shrill. "Be King!"

Poor George. He had been charmed by Lady Sarah Lennon, a delightful girl of fifteen, and yearned to marry her. But his close friend and adviser, John Stuart, Earl of Bute, sided with his mother against the match. George gave in, conceding that Bute "has thoroughly convinced me of the impropriety of marrying a country woman; the interest of my country ever shall be my first care, my own inclinations shall ever submit to it."

So George, of German stock, and speaking accented English, took a plain and proper German Protestant princess as a bride. She bore him a huge family that provided him with a minimum of pleasure and rest for all his days. As if to counter his personal discontent, George became implacable, stubborn, certain of his infallibility.

"I know I am doing my duty," he was fond of saying, "and therefore can never wish to retract."

It was this limited man, his mind blurred with hazy

ideas about kingship and his knowledge of domestic and foreign affairs meager, who came to rule at a time when events which would alter the world were taking place.

In Virginia, where tobacco was the common medium for paying taxes, the planters were hurt by the high taxes and a small harvest brought about by the French and Indian War. They prevailed upon the House of Burgesses to allow them to pay their debts in cash, at the rate of two pence per pound. With tobacco sometimes selling for as much as six pence per pound, this allowed the growers to profit by disposing of their crops when the market was strong.

It was the ministry, their salaries paid in tobacco, who objected to the Two-Penny Act. Complaints were carried to London, and the Privy Council rescinded the Two-Penny Act. This gave the Reverend James Maury of Hanover County, Virginia, cause to believe he should be paid at the old rate, or the cash equivalent, for his ministerial services. He brought suit in court.

Defending against Maury's charges was a young back-country lawyer named Patrick Henry. Aware that the members of jury were ordinary people who knew the pains of taxation, he attacked the clergy as enemies of the community. About England he said:

"Voidance of the Two-Penny Act is an infringement of Virginia's liberty. The King no longer is the father of the people. He is in fact a tyrant who forfeits all rights to his subjects' obedience."

Convinced, the jury gave Reverend Maury only one penny in damages. Here was strong evidence that the colonists were thinking more intensely about their own needs, their own rights, regardless of the wishes of their rulers in London.

Another direct challenge to British authority arose in the

Statue of King George III.

Massachusetts colony. The Navigation Acts, though seldom enforced, still stood on the books. Now, with the need for income rising, England wanted to provide customs officials with the means of gaining revenue, or seizing smuggled goods. Officials were given the power to call upon local peace officers to aid them in the search for contraband. General search warrants called Writs of Assistance were issued. These permitted officers to enter homes, shops, and storehouses in their hunt for smuggled items.

The writs were valid only during the lifetime of the king under whose rule they were issued. George II had died in 1760, and when the following year the deputy collector at Salem, Massachusetts, applied for new writs, there was opposition. Boston's merchants employed Oxenbridge Thacher and James Otis to defend their interests. The hearing took place in the Town House in Boston before five judges, bewigged and solemn in crimson robes. Members of the bar from nearby communities collected to observe and learn. Young John Adams, vitally concerned with anything that affected the welfare of the colony, was among those present.

The proceedings began with the attorney for the Crown delivering his argument in cool and measured tones. Thacher replied first, quietly persuasive, reasoned. At last it was Otis' turn. At thirty-six, he was full of energy and impatience; Adams described him later as "a flame of fire." Otis spoke in an impassioned voice.

"This writ is against the fundamental principles of law. . . . A man who is quiet, is as secure in his house, as a prince in his castle. . . . An act against the Constitution is void; an act against natural equity is void; and if an act of Parliament should be made, in the very words of this petition it would be void. The executive Courts must pass such acts into disuse."

Of Otis' speech, John Adams said: "Every man of a crowded audience appeared to me to go away, as I did, ready to take arms against writs of assistance. Then and there was the first scene of the first act of opposition to the arbitrary claims of Great Britain. Then and there the child Independence was born."

The justices would not arrive at a decision and the matter was turned over to London where authorities concluded that colonial courts could issue Writs of Assistance. But now individual Americans were questioning Parliament's right to pass any laws contrary to the English constitution, an *unwritten* body of tradition and custom and law, as interpreted, of course, by Americans themselves. Challenge to authority was becoming part of the American scene.

Typically, George III made matters worse. He issued the Royal Proclamation of 1763, which closed the newly won lands west of the Allegheny Mountains to Americans, allocating the territory to the Hudson's Bay Company. The colonists viewed this as an effort to thwart American trappers and traders. But driven by a surging spirit for expansion, they would not be checked by any law. The breach between England and her colonies widened.

4

"The art of taxation," it has been said, "consists in so plucking the goose as to obtain the largest amount of feathers with the least amount of hissing."

That was the way George Grenville would have preferred it. Grenville, England's Prime Minister since 1763, was a neat man with a precise mind, adept at recalling figures and given to avoiding rash acts. The issue of colonial taxation was simple, he decided, if only people would understand: England needed money and Americans could afford to pay a larger share than they were doing. He marshaled the facts, all the numbers, carefully studied the situation, discussed it with experts, received suggestions and reports.

Attempts were made to correct economic abuses, to claim some of the 100,000 pounds lost to the Crown each year to smugglers. The customs service was strengthened. Additional posts were created, and filled by native Englishmen, a step toward reducing unemployment and helping to balance the budget. Also, 10,000 troops were to be stationed in America (the Quartering Act), a decision made earlier. The soldiers would keep the new French and Spanish subjects in line and protect the colonies from Indian attack. Yearly cost: 350,000 pounds.

Parliament approved "An Act for the Encouragement of Officers Making Seizures," giving British naval commanders authority to apprehend suspected smugglers. Cargoes thus captured meant prize money, half of which went to the naval crews, a powerful inducement for such activity. And a supreme admiralty court was located at Halifax, site of the main British naval harbor in the hemisphere, totally removed from possible collusion with smugglers. Many reckless and unjustified seizures increased hostility between merchants and naval officers. Colonial protests were ignored.

In April 1764, the American Revenue Act, known as the Sugar Act, was passed by Parliament. In some ways it was an extension of the hated Molasses Act, but where the latter was designed to *regulate* trade, the Sugar Act was intended to raise money. Ship captains now had to post bonds insuring delivery of their cargo, thus guaranteeing the collection of duty. French wines were taxed steeply in order to increase the use of British wines, which were inferior. Silk, non-British coffee, and indigo also drew high duties.

Next came the Currency Act. This halted the issuance of bills of credit, up to now used as legal tender, and meant the colonists would have to pay their debts in hard cash.

The New York Assembly objected: ". . . if the said Plan be carried into Execution, it will not only highly reflect on the Credit, Honour, and Punctuality of this Colony, but also reduce it to a State of Bankruptcy."

Then, in March 1765, the Stamp Act became law. Stamp fees were placed on diplomas and deeds, customs papers and playing cards, newspapers and almanacs, books, advertisements, dice, bills and bonds. Since the tax itself was not heavy, and Americans were to be used to collect it, Grenville anticipated no particular objection. He was wrong. A violent storm of protest erupted along the Atlantic seaboard.

"I'll pay no such tax," a New York printer announced angrily to his friends. "Parliament would have me buy a stamp for every job I undertake, attach a stamp to every piece of paper. It will not do, gentlemen, not for a moment."

"Do we have the right to pick and choose the tax we'll pay, to decide which law to obey?"

A merchant joined the debate. "This is no abstract philosophical exchange concerning the rights of man. We have before us a practical question affecting almost every colonist."

"True," a lawyer put in. "But it is specially applicable to men like ourselves, printers, editors, shippers, merchants, for it is at us the Stamp Act is directed. Either we take an active role in opposing it, defeating it, and forcing its repeal, or we shall pay and pay and pay."

"As for me," the merchant said stubbornly, "I will pay no tax and I will import no more goods from England until the Act is done away with. And if others would act in a like fashion George III would soon come to recognize the folly of his thinking, if it be called that."

Others did follow his lead, and soon British merchants

began to feel the effect of a diminishing business. Colonial objections continued to grow stronger, louder, more daring.

In Virginia's House of Burgesses, on a sultry day in May, Patrick Henry rose to speak against the Stamp Act, to present seven resolves. A fiery radical, intensely ambitious, he was a flamboyant speaker and his words had a searing effect.

"Caesar had his Brutus," he cried dramatically, "Charles the First his Cromwell; and George the Third—"

"Treason!" some of his listeners shouted.

"—and George the Third," Henry went on, "may profit by their example. If this be treason, make the most of it."

Henry's resolves underscored the rights of the colonists to be taxed "by themselves, or by persons chosen to represent them . . . governed by such laws as are derived from their own consent . . ." The spirit of opposition grew, and protest was heard throughout the colonies.

Angered by these restrictive laws, the colonists formed groups called Sons of Liberty. Vocal protests were not enough for many of these men, some of whom were debtors and saw an opportunity to better their personal conditions in chaos. In Boston, there was mob action, the Sons of Liberty attacking the house of Andrew Oliver, named as a stamp distributor. The young women of Rhode Island declared that they would reject the attentions of any suitor favoring the Stamp Act. Another mob stormed the house of Thomas Hutchinson, lieutenant governor of Massachusetts. Such acts were duplicated in North Carolina, Delaware, and New York.

More orderly and purposeful action also began to take place. The Stamp Act Congress met in New York with twenty-seven delegates from nine colonies attending. Georgia, Virginia, North Carolina, and New Hampshire sent no delegates, but the assemblies of these colonies signified "that

they would agree to whatever was done by the Congress."

Though there was no unanimity, the Congress did display a growing sense of mutual interest. The delegates began to realize that what affected one colony affected the others as well. They declared the recurring theme that Englishmen in America possessed the same rights as those in the mother country and were not to be taxed without their consent. They came out against the system which tried citizens without juries in admiralty courts, maintaining that every Englishman was entitled to a trial by a jury of his peers.

This Congress marked the first truly representative assembly of colonials working for the common good. It made clear the widespread opposition to the Stamp Act. Memorials, resolutions, petitions, meetings, and riots all followed to emphasize that stand. The Stamp Act, designed to raise money, had the reverse effect.

English products went unsold. Debts went unpaid and orders were canceled, throwing thousands of Englishmen out of work. Severe damage was done to British commerce, and London's merchants appealed to the government for help.

Parliament decided to explore the matter. Early in 1766 Benjamin Franklin appeared before the House of Commons to present the colonial point of view. Here was no fiery radical, no hot-eyed revolutionary, but the Postmaster General of North America, a stout, genial fellow with a benign smile and bright eyes behind steel-rimmed spectacles. Even his clothes were reassuring: he wore a plum-colored coat and knee breeches, a ruffled shirt and a silk waistcoat, white stockings and conservatively buckled shoes. His wig was properly powdered.

A member of the House asked Franklin if the people of

America would pay the stamp tax if it were modified.

Franklin smiled a little sadly. "No, never, unless compelled by force of arms."

A suppressed uneasiness trickled through the hall.

"Can anything less than a military force carry the stamp act into execution?"

"I do not see how a military force can be applied to that purpose," was Franklin's reasoned reply.

"Why may it not?"

"Suppose a military force sent into America, they will find nobody in arms; what are they then to do? They cannot force a man to take stamps who chooses to do without them. They will not find a rebellion; they may indeed make one."

Franklin had made his point clear—the Stamp Act was unenforceable, its hoped-for duties uncollectable. The rapidly worsening situation had to be remedied.

One member of Parliament, a merchant, contacted the new Prime Minister, the young and inexperienced Lord Charles Rockingham. "Our trade is hurt," he emphasized. "What the devil have you been doing? For our part, we don't pretend to understand your politics and American matters, but our trade is hurt; pray remedy it, and plague you if you won't."

Others felt similarly, foremost among them William Pitt, the Great Commoner. Ill and unsteady, he rose to address the House of Commons, his manner impatient and his voice full of scorn.

"I rejoice that America has resisted," he thundered. "The gentleman asks, when were the colonies emancipated? But I desire to know, when were they made slaves? . . . Upon the whole, I will beg leave to tell the House what is really my opinion. It is, that the Stamp Act be repealed absolutely, totally, and immediately."

And repealed it was, in March 1766. At the same time, the duty on molasses was reduced to one penny a gallon. There was rejoicing in America. The happy colonists managed to overlook the Declaratory Act which Parliament passed on the same day the Stamp Act was repealed. This act made clear the lesser position of the colonies and England's right to deal with them accordingly. It said in part:

> That the said colonies . . . have been, are, and of right ought to be, subordinate unto, and dependent upon the imperial crown and parliament of Great Britain; and that the King's majesty . . . in parliament assembled, had, hath, and of right ought to have, full power and authority to make laws and statutes . . . to bind the colonies and people of America . . . in all cases whatsoever.

In England, changes occurred. George III grew weary of Rockingham's ministry and wanted to replace him with William Pitt. Meanwhile, Lord Grafton was nominal head of the government. It seemed to some people on both sides of the Atlantic that the time of trouble was past. Others were less optimistic, among them Samuel Adams.

A familiar figure in Boston, Sam Adams was paunchy and puritanical, given to puffing on a white clay pipe—a fiery, courageous man concerned with justice and right. A political creature, he cared little for other matters, and met often in a private room behind the Salutation Tavern in caucus with such other Sons of Liberty as James Otis, the silversmith Paul Revere, Dr. Joseph Warren, and his own second cousin, John Adams.

Gifted with a fine command of language, clerk to the General Court, Sam Adams enjoyed writing letters on political affairs to prominent men throughout the colonies. And, under a variety of pen names, he wrote for local newspapers, scratching away with quill and ink until the early morning hours. He was palsied and his hair was gray, his mouth frequently trembled and he spoke in a voice thin and shrill. Hardly an intimidating person, yet he was characterized as being among Boston's foremost troublemakers.

"I doubt," Thomas Hutchinson, a member of the governor's council, said, "whether there is a greater incendiary in the King's dominions or a man of greater malignity of heart; or who less scruples any measure ever so criminal to accomplish his purposes."

Whether patriot or villain, Sam Adams was able to see things as they were, never to lose sight of distant goals. He claimed that repeal of the Stamp Act provided only a temporary respite for the colonists, that economic conditions in England and the antiquated political thinking of her leaders made some new and equally oppressive law inevitable. Events proved him right.

In England, William Pitt fell ill. Someone had to assume control of the government. It was Charles Townshend, Chancellor of the Exchequer, an outstanding debater, occasionally brilliant, popularly known as "Champagne Charlie," who happily volunteered.

He took note of the high cost of living in England, the general dissatisfaction with the situation in America, and determined to do something about both. He promptly sliced four hundred thousand pounds from the government's income by reducing the land tax. How was that considerable sum to be replaced? Townshend had an answer: America would pay; and at the same time he intended to administer a lesson in manners to the colonial upstarts.

Townshend's formula was simple. Impose duties on certain items: tea, paper, paint, lead, glass; the customs service

Samuel Adams.

would be reorganized to collect the taxes in America. A supervisory Board of Customs Commissioners was to be located in Boston, the heart of most colonial unrest. A portion of the funds raised would be used to pay the officials who enforced the new laws, thus weakening the dominion of colonial assemblies over them. Violators would be tried *without* a jury.

Further, the New York Assembly, which had yet to comply with the billeting requirements of the Quartering Act, was suspended.

Colonists reacted hotly to the Townshend Acts. Sam Adams had been right: repeal of the Stamp Act resolved nothing. The fight had to go on. Once again people began to make clear their preference for homemade products, and they rejected foreign luxuries, including tea. Merchants agreed to halt British importations until the situation was altered.

John Dickinson, a successful lawyer and farmer, educated in England, published a series of articles called "Letters from a Farmer in Pennsylvania." He insisted that Parliament's efforts to raise revenue in the colonies were unconstitutional, challenging the Declaratory Act, attacking the Townshend Acts, claiming Americans would "be drained of the rewards of their labor, to cherish the scorching sands of Florida and the icy rocks of Canada and Nova Scotia, which will never return to us one farthing that we send them." He characterized suspension of the New York Assembly as "violation of the liberty" of that colony, insisting that "the cause of one is the cause of all," calling for all the colonies to band together into "one body politic." Here again in time of stress was a cry for colonial unity.

In February 1768, Sam Adams was the motivating force in drafting the Massachusetts Circular Letter, dispatched to legislatures throughout the colonies. It too made a plea for unity, ending with an affirmation of loyalty to the Crown. Even the most fiery of Americans were not talking revolution or independence, insisting only on their rights as Englishmen under English rule.

In August, Boston approved a Non-Importation Agreement—no goods were to be brought in from England. Later that same month, New York's merchants signed a similar pact, but it was to be a full year later before Philadelphia joined them in the boycott. In the South, interest in such activities was minimal until gradually the idea took hold that the cause of New England was indeed the cause of every colony.

The Virginia Resolves of May 1769 spoke out for taxation only by one's own representatives. This aroused the resident governor to such a pitch that he dissolved the House of Burgesses. Infuriated by the action, the leaders of that body, Peyton Randolph, Thomas Jefferson, George Washington, Patrick Henry, and Richard Henry Lee, called for a special convention to endorse a non-importation agreement. The remainder of the South approved.

Provocations came from both sides. James Otis, opposing the actions of customs officials, was attacked and seriously wounded by a blow from a sword. The Sons of Liberty destroyed a revenue ship off Newport; and a customs commissioner was tarred and feathered in Providence. In Boston, a group of citizens dragged a customs man from his home, and in self-defense he used his pistol, killing a young boy. In New York, opposing mobs fought in what was called the Battle of Golden Hill.

When two minor customs officials appeared below decks on John Hancock's ship *Lydia,* they were promptly and not too gently deposited topside. The Customs Department tried to bring suit against Hancock, but the Attorney General maintained he had been within his rights. However, the matter was not yet ended.

Hancock's sloop, *Liberty,* put into Boston Harbor with twenty-five casks of Madeira wine aboard, paid the required duty, and took on a fresh cargo of whale oil and tar. Technically, before loading began a bond should have been posted, but usual procedure was to put up the bond when ships cleared out of port. The *Liberty* was seized and Hancock arrested, charged with evasion of taxes, and heavily fined. With John Adams as his lawyer, Hancock came to trial, but the Crown's case was so weak that it was finally dropped. Hancock never regained possession of the *Liberty*.

In London, action was called for. The previous December, Charles Townshend had died and his place had been taken by Lord North, a stubborn, unimaginative man, anxious to uphold the dignity of the Crown at any cost. To do so he created a new post, Secretariat of State, its function to deal with colonial matters exclusively. The job was given to Lord Hillsborough, a pompous man who shared North's conviction that the colonials sought nothing less than total independence. They agreed that Americans should be taught a lesson, and ordered some of their best teachers overseas— regular British soldiers.

Redcoats in the colonies aggravated the situation. In New York, when "Liberty poles" were erected, the soldiers chopped them down. Others rose swiftly into place. Even George Washington, a calm man not given to rash statements, spoke for freedom.

"No man," he said, "should hesitate a moment to use arms in defence of so valuable a blessing."

But first blood would not be shed in Virginia. Nor in New York. That would happen in Boston on an icy March

5, 1770. Snow had fallen that morning and into the afternoon. As evening came on the skies cleared and the moon reflected off the white streets.

There was a restlessness in the city, and small bands of men roamed about looking for excitement, or for trouble. In Dock Square, an unidentified bewigged man in a red cape harangued a crowd on the inequities of British law and the restrictive influence of British troops.

British soldiers in Boston found hostility at every turn. They were insulted and tormented and could not respond, being under orders to restrain themselves. Poorly paid, and with nothing to do, the soldiers were irritable and showed little goodwill toward the colonists.

At about eight o'clock Captain John Goldfinch was walking along King Street on his way to the barracks. He was intercepted by a barber's apprentice, young Edward Garrick, who demanded to know why Goldfinch hadn't paid his hairdressing bill. Goldfinch responded by striking the boy, then moving on, the incident closed as far as he was concerned.

It wasn't. About an hour later, a crowd came surging out of Royal Exchange Lane into King Street and spotted the sentinel, Hugh White, in front of the customs house.

"Here's the soldier who struck the barber's boy!" someone cried.

"Kill the lobster! Kill the soldier!"

"Coward! Knock him down!"

At once White was pelted with rock-centered snowballs. Frightened and confused, he primed his musket.

"Go ahead, shoot!" the mob challenged, confident that no British soldier would dare shoot another Englishman without authorization of a civilian magistrate. And what magistrate would dare issue such an order? They became increasingly abusive, more aggressive.

The bell in the steeple of Old South Church began to toll, and, as if on signal, more people came rushing into the square. Up from the wharfs came a gang of harbor toughs.

White was rattled. He scurried back up the steps of the customs house. The crowd pressed forward, jeering, throwing snowballs and chunks of wood. He called for help, and Captain Thomas Preston led a sergeant and six privates to the scene. Relieved to see them, White moved back down the steps.

Captain Preston maneuvered himself between the mob and his men, trying to reason with the colonists. They ignored his pleas to disband, to return to their homes. The nine soldiers were faced by at least a hundred angry Bostonians who continued to hurl everything at hand.

"Lobsters! Bloody backs! You dare not fire! Burn the sentry box!"

It became confused after that. Crispus Attucks, a big man, part Negro, part Indian, moved forward to wave his club menacingly at Hugh White. A soldier was struck by a thrown object. Perhaps he lost his balance, or dropped his rifle, or maybe Attucks tried to wrench White's rifle away from him. In any case, a shot rang out and Attucks fell over dead. The mob came on; clubs were swung and more shots fired. Alarm drums beat out and reinforcements came hurrying from the barracks, bayonets glinting in the moonlight.

Thomas Hutchinson, now lieutenant governor, appeared on the balcony of the State House. The sight that met his eyes sent a shiver of apprehension down his spine. Civilians and soldiers faced each other across the street, each defiant, waiting for the next outbreak of violence.

"Go home!" he cried. "Go home and leave this to the authorities. The law will settle the matter. Go home before

The Boston Massacre on King Street.

more blood is spilled. I promise you, there will be an inquiry."

Slowly, very slowly, the mob broke up, disappeared, the trouble over for that night. Five Americans—Crispus Attucks, Samuel Gray, James Caldwell, Samuel Maverick, Patrick Carr—died as a result of the violence, and six more were wounded. That night would not be forgotten.

5

The Boston Massacre failed to stir colonists outside that city to take up arms against England. Yet, as if in response to it, though such was not at all the case, Parliament repealed the Townshend Act with a single exception, the duty on tea. By its continuance, King and Parliament both affirmed the Declaratory Act.

Said George III: "I am clear there must always be one tax to keep the right, and as such I approve the Tea Duty."

Soon much of the traditional feeling of goodwill returned. Non-importation agreements were forgotten and merchants again began to buy British. In the three years that followed, business was excellent, and there was little talk about constitutional rights. Tea was brought into the colonies and taxes paid on it without argument. And the same for molasses.

Prosperous and at peace, many colonists felt they had won a partial victory of principle and self-interest; they had no desire to stir up unwanted trouble. It was good to be a part of the British Empire, rewarding in many ways, secure, and they wanted to remain so. But events and men conspired against them.

Colonial radicals were opposed to further trade with England. Sam Adams held that the "democratical" progress of America would end unless agitation continued. Even his cousin John was disturbed by the trend toward conciliation. And as if determined to keep the colonial pot at a boil, the British made a serious error. They failed to abolish the American Board of Customs Commissioners, men anxious to line their own pockets and commanding several warships with which to do so.

They tried to stop the smuggling of tea, and diligently extracted tolls from the small boats that plied the coastal waters transporting provisions and wood. The schooner *Gaspee,* commanded by Lieutenant William Dudingston, was particularly active in the area of Narragansett Bay, seizing and searching in a manner arrogant, painful, and costly. The *Gaspee* had great success until it set out after a swift packet one day, running aground off Namquit Point.

That night eight boatloads of colonists approached the *Gaspee,* boarded her, and took the crew prisoner. After the crew was put into their boats, the *Gaspee* was set afire. Subsequently, an investigation was made by a royal commission which took depositions. When the commission adjourned it had discovered only that no one in Rhode Island appeared to know anything about the affair.

The incident provided great impetus to Committees of Correspondence, which had come into being earlier. These were formed in order to keep Americans throughout the colonies informed. The driving force behind the Committees was Sam Adams, and by using swift horsemen he had established a communication chain which went far to forge a sense of unity among the thirteen colonies.

It was the aim of the Committees to emphasize colonial rights and at the same time detail all violations of those rights, so that they worked as an extension of the Sons of Liberty. Sam Adams wrote the initial report of the Boston Committee in characteristically strong language: "The colonists have been branded with the odious names of traitors and rebels, only for complaining of their grievances; how long such treatment will, or ought to be borne, is submitted." It was increasingly evident that Sam Adams, at least, wanted to move Massachusetts nearer to independence.

Unwittingly, the English were his most effective allies.

Early in 1773, the East India Company came upon hard times. Its stock had been halved in value, and it owed the Crown great sums of money. Since many members of Parliament owned shares in the company, they were intent on saving it, and themselves, from financial disaster. The House of Commons passed a bill extending permission to the company to sell seventeen million pounds of tea, in storage in London, directly to America.

The tea was available with no duties or custom charges in England, but subject to a three-penny per pound tax in the colonies. Though Americans had always paid a levy on tea, they objected to this one and to the advantage it provided the company which would be able to sell its product cheaper than its competitors. They also objected to the fact that only certain favored English merchants would be allowed to sell this tea, an arrangement which raised the ghost of monopoly, something all colonial merchants opposed. Once accepted, they pointed out, monopoly could be expanded to take in such products as foodstuffs, grain, cloth, shoes.

Joseph Reed of Philadelphia said, "Those who are in trade have the additional motive of interest, and dread a monopoly whose extent may destroy one third of their business. For India goods compose one third of our importations from England."

The business methods and attitudes of the East India Company added to the offensive nature of the matter. Protests reached such a feverish pitch in New York and Philadelphia that the King's agent in both cities resigned.

Nevertheless, the East India Company dispatched shiploads of tea to a number of American ports. The Sons of Liberty took note of this and posted the following resolution in New York City:

That whoever shall aid, or abet, or in any manner assist in the introduction of tea from any place whatsoever, into this colony, while it is subject, by the British act to Parliament, to the payment of a duty, for the purpose of raising a revenue in America, he shall be deemed an enemy to the liberties of America.

The tea arrived in New York and Philadelphia and was unloaded, and promptly reloaded onto ships returning to England. In Charleston, the tea was quickly stored out of sight. Customs officials, wary of the rising public temper, chose to take no action.

The situation in Boston was different.

Tea was on its way to Boston in three vessels, the *Dartmouth,* the *Eleanor,* and the *Beaver.* Sons of Liberty made ready to greet them. Meetings were held, speeches delivered, protests made. Delegations visited those merchants to whom the tea was consigned—the two sons of Governor Hutchinson, Richard Clarke, Benjamin Faneuil, Jr., and Joshua Winslow. Important men, they refused to be intimidated.

On the morning of November 3, Boston woke to find handbills posted all over town. They read:

To the Freemen of this and the neighboring towns.

GENTLEMEN,—You are desired to meet at Liberty Tree, this day, at twelve o'clock at noon; and then and there to hear the persons to whom the tea shipped by the East-India Company is consigned, make a public resignation of their office as consignors upon oath; and also swear that they will re-ship any teas that may be consigned to them by said company by the first vessel sailing for London.

A crowd gathered, but the consignees did not appear. Sam Adams addressed the crowd, excoriating the Tea Act; and then the angry men marched to the store of Richard Clarke, insisting he refuse the tea. When he rejected their demands, they wrecked his home.

On November 28, the *Dartmouth* sailed into the harbor, 114 chests of tea in her hold. The ship moored at Long Wharf, and a guard was posted by the Sons of Liberty to make sure no tea was unloaded. A meeting was held in Old South Church the next day, and there were more speeches and more resolutions. The *Dartmouth* was moved to a new anchor at Griffin's Wharf, where, a few days later, it was joined by the *Eleanor* and the *Beaver,* each laden with tea.

"The ships must go!" Sam Adams insisted, and his audience agreed. Even Quaker Francis Rotch, who had leased the *Dartmouth,* was for sending her back unloaded. It was not to be. Governor Hutchinson refused permission for the return voyage. He ordered two warships to guard the harbor's exit and commanded the guns of Castle William be made ready to fire.

On December 16, at ten in the morning, some seven thousand irate Bostonians gathered at Old South Church, despite a thin, chilling mist. They waited all day for a message from Hutchinson that he had changed his mind, would release the tea. At last word came. Hutchinson was adamant; the tea would stay.

Sam Adams shoved himself erect, lumbered up to the pulpit. An uneasy silence descended. "This meeting," he said in a loud voice, "can do nothing more to save the country."

His words carried outside to where some fifty men, faces stained with lampblack and dressed in Indian costumes, waited. They carried tomahawks and axes and knives, and they began to whoop and holler as they headed for Griffin's Wharf. The crowd surged after them to watch the fun.

The "Indians" boarded the three moored ships and carted the tea chests topside, where they were broken open, the contents dumped into Boston Harbor. By nine o'clock the work was done, eighteen thousand pounds of tea destroyed. Nothing else was touched and there was no disorder.

In April 1774, New Yorkers followed Boston's lead with a tea party of their own.

Of the Boston Tea Party, John Adams said: "This is the most significant movement of all. There is dignity, a majesty, a sublimity, in this last effort of the patriots that I greatly admire. This destruction of the tea is so bold, so firm, intrepid and inflexible, and it must have important consequences, and so lasting that I cannot but consider it as an epoch in history."

In England, a hot debate broke out, and there were cries in Parliament that Boston must not go unpunished. Lord North said, "The test of the Bostonians will not be the indemnification of the East India Company alone; it will remain in the breast of the King not to restore the port until peace and obedience shall be observed in the port of Boston."

Another member of Parliament said: "I am of the opinion that you will never meet with that proper obedience to the laws of this country until you have destroyed that nest of locusts."

Edmund Burke raised his voice against intemperate action, attempted to answer passion with reason. "Repeal, Sir, the Act which gave rise to this disturbance; this will be the remedy to bring peace and quietness and restore authority; but a great black book and a great many red coats will never be able to govern it. It is true, the Americans cannot resist the force of this country, but it will cause wranglings, scuffling and discontent. Such remedies as the foregoing will create disturbances that can never be quieted."

The voice of reason did not prevail. Parliament moved to punish Boston, passing a series of laws known as the Coercive or the Intolerable Acts, aimed specifically at that city. First, the port was closed to all commerce, all shipping, until the destroyed tea was paid for in full. Next, the Massachusetts charter was revoked. Town meetings were forbidden unless consented to by the governor. Another provision stated that any customs official, soldier, or magistrate in-

Destruction of tea in Boston Harbor.

dicted for a capital offense within the colony could be tried in Nova Scotia, or in England, rather than submit to a jury of hostile natives. And, once again, troops were to be quartered in Boston. To enforce these acts, General Gage was appointed governor.

Writing of the Boston Port Act, Sam Adams said:

> Our business is to find means to evade its malignant design. The inhabitants view it not with astonishment, but with indignation. They discover the utmost contempt of the framers of it . . . I trust in God this devoted town will sustain the shock with dignity; and, supported by their brethren, will gloriously defeat the designs of their common enemies . . . We will endeavour, by circumspection and sound prudence, to frustrate the diabolical designs of our enemies.

The various colonies began sending provisions to beleaguered Boston. Meat, fish, and oil came from towns close at hand; the Carolinas sent rice and other victuals; Connecticut sent sheep; Pennsylvania flour. Money came from all of them. And resolutions of sympathy were passed in New York, in Williamsburg, in Philadelphia.

Of this mounting unity, General Gage commented: "I find they [the Bostonians] have some warm friends in New York and Philadelphia . . . that the people of Charleston are as mad as they are . . . This province is supported and abetted by others beyond the conception of most people, and foreseen by none."

He was right. The colonists were men with a mission, a mission whose time had come.

6

Colonial discontent spread and intensified. The Intolerable Acts, the shifting of the capital of Massachusetts from Boston to Salem, the tax on tea, all were discussed and argued, a catalogue of complaints about which something had to be done. And once more the doing began in the Bay Colony. Behind a locked-door meeting in Salem, Sam Adams presiding, it was resolved that all the colonies should meet to consult on what was being done and what could be done in the future in order that they might move closer to the "recovery and establishment of just rights and liberties, civil and religious, and the restoration of union and harmony between Great Britain and the colonies, most ardently desired by all good men."

Word went out. Philadelphia was to be the site for this meeting, the First Continental Congress. In the heat of August they traveled, fifty-six delegates from twelve colonies, Georgia alone not represented. Men of all political shadings were represented: radicals such as Patrick Henry and the Adamses; conservatives Joseph Galloway of Pennsylvania and John Rutledge of South Carolina; and the "mongrels," as John Adams termed them, men like Washington, whose opinion fell somewhere between the extremes.

There were two notable absentees: Benjamin Franklin, then in England, and Thomas Jefferson, at home in Virginia. The Congress commenced on September 5; and, though there was universal support for the meeting, there was considerable difference of opinion when it came to specific issues.

Said John Adams: "Fifty gentlemen meeting together, all strangers, are not acquainted with each other's language, ideas, views, designs. They are therefore jealous of each other—fearful, timid, skittish."

Gradually, they came to know each other at meetings, at dinner or over a tankard of ale, at gatherings of different sorts. Soon they learned that no matter what colony they came from there was much that bound them, an abiding mutuality of interest.

Caesar Rodney of Delaware said of the Bostonians he met: ". . . condemned by many for their violence [they] are moderate men when compared to Virginia, South Carolina, and Rhode Island."

Silas Deane of Connecticut could write that "he had never met, nor scarcely had an idea of meeting, with men of such firmness, sensibility, spirit, and thorough knowledge of the interests of America, as the Gentlemen from the Southern Provinces . . ."

The delegates set to work. No one labored harder or more diligently than Sam Adams. He coaxed and argued, wheedled and declaimed, making his presence felt in all places.

"He eats little," Joseph Galloway of Pennsylvania said, "drinks little, sleeps little, thinks much and is most decisive and indefatigable in the pursuit of his objects."

Adams wanted congressional approval of the resolves adopted by Suffolk County, Massachusetts, opposing the Intolerable Acts. The resolves stated that "the people owed an indispensable duty to God and to their country to preserve those liberties for which the fathers had fought and bled."

Despite the opposition of conservatives, who feared the resolves might end all hope of reconciliation with England, they were approved.

"This day convinced me," John Adams said, "that America will support Massachusetts or perish with her."

A gloomy Joseph Galloway rose to claim that they had now erected "the foundation of military resistance . . ." He introduced a conciliatory plan.

Patrick Henry took the floor. "Government is dissolved," he insisted dramatically. "Where are your landmarks, your boundaries of colonies: We are in a state of nature . . . The distinction between Virginians, Pennsylvanians, New Yorkers, and New Englanders are no more. I am not a Virginian, but an American."

The Galloway Plan was rejected. Soon after, Paul Revere came galloping into Philadelphia with word from Boston. General Gage had dissolved the Massachusetts Assembly and was establishing military fortifications in the city. Did Gage intend to hold the citizens of Boston as hostages in order to force obedience to parliamentary law?

This uncertainty and fear was expressed in a Declaration of Rights and Grievances. In ten resolutions the colonies professed their continuing loyalty to the Crown. But they questioned Parliament's control over them. They were convinced that such authority should be, and by all rights was, limited only to the supervision of external trade, and then only so that they might secure "the commercial advantages of the Empire."

Out of this Congress came the Continental Association. It was dedicated to non-importation of English goods, to keeping prices down, to surveying customs houses, to effecting boycotts, and to spreading the "truth." All of this served only to excite passions in England and to raise the spectre of colonial revolt. It also caused George III to become increasingly conscious of his kingly duties.

"The dye is now cast," he declared. "The Colonies must either submit or triumph; I do not wish to come to severer measures, but we must not retreat."

Parliament promptly declared Massachusetts to be in a state of rebellion and ordered such rebellion put down. In a move calculated to end disobedience in Boston, and elsewhere, the military command of that city was increased to ten thousand men.

Then came the First Restraining Act. Designed as a punitive measure, it limited the trade of New England and forbade fishermen from working the Grand Banks, their primary source of a catch. When this failed to have the desired result, a Second Restraining Act was passed to include all the other colonies except New York, North Carolina, and Georgia, in the hope of influencing the latter to remain loyal.

In both countries, men of goodwill worked for compromise, for a conciliatory solution. Eloquence and logic fell short of what was required, for passions were inflamed on both sides.

When word reached General Gage that military supplies were being stored at Cambridge and Charlestown, he sent out raiding parties. Anti-British sentiment grew more feverish.

This was precisely what many radicals desired. Rumors spread from town to town, house to house, suggesting widespread violence and destruction by the troops. Before long thousands of armed Massachusetts men were hurrying toward Cambridge to oppose the redcoats.

General Gage was distressed. "I want peace," he told his officers. "It is not my intention to make war upon these Englishmen." He ordered additional men into the field to disperse the colonials, to reassure them about his intentions. Gage continued to make efforts to quiet the population, even to asking those two "rebellious" fellows, John Hancock and Samuel Adams, to help calm the citizenry.

It was too late for such piecemeal measures. People were moving to improve their military posture. Money was raised to buy arms and ammunition. The militia was reorganized and new officers appointed. Food was gathered and stored in safe places, and entire families put in long hours casting bullets. Along the coast, gunrunning was continual; and four cannon were stolen from Boston Common and more from the British battery at Charlestown.

Gage was anxious to stop such activities, and, when he heard from British sympathizers (Tories, as those who favored England were called) that there were field cannon at Salem, he sent a detachment to capture them. But the villagers had been warned, and when the soldiers arrived it was to find a large and well-armed contingent of farmers and townspeople waiting. There was nothing to do but return empty handed.

Nor was the situation elsewhere much better. In Virginia, such aggressively intemperate language was hurled about that Gage decided the men of that colony really did want war. Patrick Henry said it for so many others when he spoke before the House of Burgesses:

"We must fight! I repeat it, sir, we must fight! An appeal to arms and to the God of Hosts is all that is left us . . . Gentlemen may cry, peace, peace—but there is no peace. The war is actually begun! The next gale that sweeps from the north will bring to our ears the clash of resounding arms! Our brethren are already in the field! Why stand we here idle? What is it that gentlemen wish? What would they have? Is life so dear, or peace so sweet, as to be purchased at the price of chains and slavery? Forbid it, Almighty God! I know not what course others may take; but as for me, give me liberty, or give me death!"

Not every colonist felt that way, and there was considerable pamphleteering against rebellion. A series of letters by an Anglican minister, Samuel Seabury, included these words: "People who talk so feelingly, and with so much pleasure about revolutions, and who are ever ready to justify the most violent and the most needless opposition to government . . . seem to me too fond of revolution to be good subjects of any government on earth. . . . If we must be enslaved, let it be by a King at least, and not by a parcel of upstart, lawless committeemen."

It was too late for such an argument to prevail. Emotions ran too high, and too many steps away from compromise had been taken, too many harsh denunciations made. Action begat reaction. Threats drew counterthreats. Pride in one side stimulated it in the opposition.

Patrick Henry delivering his great "liberty or death" speech before the Virginia Assembly.

General Gage, prodded by communications from London, taunted by Tories, urged to extinguish the smoldering rebellion, decided to act. He knew that at Concord, only eighteen miles from Boston, military supplies had been hidden. He issued orders that they be destroyed. He also called for the arrest of John Hancock and Sam Adams, the latter in hiding near Lexington.

Gage's strategy was simple—under cover of darkness an infantry regiment and some grenadiers would be ferried across the bay to East Cambridge. Once ashore, they would march with all speed that good order allowed. Earlier, he had ordered soldiers to clear the road out of Cambridge, hoping to prevent Yankee messengers from alerting the people of Concord.

It was a futile effort. That same night couriers Paul Revere, William Dawes, and Dr. Samuel Prescott galloped out with the news, alerting the countryside.

The British force, eight hundred strong, commanded by Lieutenant Colonel Francis Smith, marched through the night. But stealth was no longer required. All along the route they heard the booming of cannon, the sharp crack of muskets, the sound of church bells, all signaling their approach.

At Lexington, Massachusetts men assembled on the common about midnight, shivering in chill air of that April 18. They milled about, murmuring their concerns, seeking to support each other's courage. After a while, since nothing was happening, some of them went home to bed. Others moved into the tavern to continue the wait under pleasanter circumstances. No one was sure what they were waiting for, or what they were supposed to do. Talk among friends of freedom and opposition to tyranny was one thing; opposing trained and battle-hardened British troops, the world's best fighters, was something entirely different. Yet they waited.

They were well into the morning hours when a rider, Thaddeus Bowman, came galloping up. "They're coming!" he shouted. "They're almost here!"

There was no hesitation. Men snatched up their muskets and rushed out onto the green, seventy of them, commanded by Captain John Parker. He managed to form them into two thin lines. They stood uncertainly, glancing sidelong at each other. Dawn streaked the eastern sky and the first gray light lent an eerie cast to the green. William Diamond rattled out a drumbeat; at eighteen, he was eager, but frightened.

At last they heard it: the cadence of marching men. Parker checked his men, all in ranks on the green. Good. The road was open and he would do nothing to close it, nothing to trigger a fight. To make a show of force would be enough.

"We have no war here," he warned. "Do not fire unless fired upon."

The advance column of British appeared, marines in charge of Major John Pitcairn. He galloped forward, flanked by two captains, a handsome trio in colorful uniforms, swords gleaming, wigs powdered white. He called on the Americans to lay down their arms, to disperse.

Suddenly all was chaos. Behind Pitcairn, the redcoats, drawn tight by continued abuse over a long period of time, broke ranks and charged, cheering and shouting as they came. Pitcairn wheeled his mount around, signaled frantically for the men to halt, to re-form and resume normal discipline.

Parker had not anticipated this. Bearing down on him was an overwhelming force, and he commanded only seventy men. He ordered them to fall back. But it was too late.

The Battle of Lexington.

A shot rang out. As if a prearranged signal, it drew a volley from British muskets, to be answered by the colonists. Men toppled over.

Major Pitcairn was frantic. "Stop!" he cried, trying to penetrate the din. "Stop firing!"

At last the officers regained control of their troops and the shooting ended. Eight Americans were dead, ten more wounded—out of resentment and confusion and misunderstanding, an almost accidental spark setting off the American Revolution. Yet it had also been a long time coming. The fallen minutemen had died out of devotion to a set of principles which they believed would protect their rights and their freedom.

An hour later, the British troops resumed their march toward Concord, sounding a triumphant cheer, pleased with their morning's work. Before they made it back to Boston, they would lose all zest for cheering.

7

At Concord, a sentry marched glumly in front of the courthouse. His name was Amos Melven and he had been stationed there by Colonel James Barrett, commander of the Concord militia. Melven's orders were simple—if anything unusual occurred he was to pull the bell rope, sound the alarm. Such a waste of time. Nothing was happening. Nothing would happen, of that he was sure. One more long, dull afternoon. He would be pleased when his tour of duty ended.

A horseman appeared; Melven paid him no attention. It was Dr. Prescott making his usual Tuesday visit to pay court to a lady living in Lexington. But Prescott came galloping past the millpond and into the square, reining to a stop, words tumbling from his lips. Melven tried to make sense out of them.

"The bell, man. Ring the bell. There's been a battle at Lexington and the regulars are coming. Ring the bell!"

Melven blanched, and ran for the bell rope. The warning pealed out, alerting the men of Concord. With muskets and pistols, they headed for Wright's Tavern, the assembly point. William Emerson, a clergyman, was the first to arrive. Next came Colonel Barrett. And all the others, anxious, perhaps, but ready to do what was necessary. A scout went out, Reuben Brown. Soon men began arriving from other towns: Sudbury, Dedham, Andover, Worcester, Woburn, Lynn, Billerica, and Lincoln.

Presently Reuben Brown returned to confirm Prescott's report. Barrett listened solemnly, then issued orders. The shooting at Lexington had come about almost accidentally. Here things would be different. The men of Concord were going to stand and fight.

It was eight o'clock that night when the British arrived at Concord. Colonel Smith and Major Pitcairn studied the situation. Information had come to them that beyond North Bridge, over the Concord River, at the farm of James Barrett, a large cache of arms were hidden. Orders were snapped out.

Three companies went marching across North Bridge in precise ranks. Even as they did, from the heights above the bridge there appeared a loose formation of farmers and shopkeepers, merchants and beardless youths, trying without much success to keep step to the tempo of "The White Cockade" as played by the Acton fifers.

Once on the road, they swung in the direction of the

bridge, toward the oncoming redcoats. Commands were given, and the colonists charged. A shot was fired, another, a wild fusillade. Abner Hosmer, from Acton, fell dead. And Isaac Davis. Still they came on, firing as they advanced. Nine redcoats died and three more were wounded.

The British hesitated, stopped, milled about in confusion. One man took a backward step and at once the soldiers were moving off the bridge, retreating toward the safety of Concord. For them, there was no safety. Hundreds of farmers had converged on the area, and now they subjected the troops to a deadly attack from all sides. Colonel Smith ordered his men to pull out of Concord.

No orderly retreat was possible. All along the line of march they were peppered by musket fire. Every tree, it seemed, every stone wall, every ditch concealed an armed Yankee. Soldiers continued to fall. Only the arrival of reinforcements saved the situation from becoming a total disaster. The British suffered an estimated 273 casualties, the Americans ninety-five. These were the shots "heard round the world."

The American Revolution had begun.

News of the "victories" at Lexington and Concord was carried by horsemen throughout the colonies. Many Americans hesitant about the colonial cause up to now joined in. Men everywhere made ready to fight.

In Connecticut, Benedict Arnold called for recruits to form an army; Nathanael Greene recruited men in Rhode Island; and John Stark did likewise in New Hampshire. George Washington said that for Americans the choice now was simple—war or slavery. And in South Carolina, two regiments were quickly organized.

At the same time, delegates to the Second Continental Congress were making their way toward Philadelphia.

When, on May 10, 1775, they convened, it was to discover that all the colonies favored giving Massachusetts every possible assistance.

Nevertheless, unity was difficult to come by. John Adams complained later, "Every step was opposed and carried by bare majorities."

Though some delegates still yearned to re-establish harmony with England, it was clear to them all that defensive measures were necessary. It was decided that twelve companies of riflemen would be raised in Virginia, Maryland, and Pennsylvania, the beginnings of a Continental Army. On June 15, Congress declared "That a General be appointed to command all the continental forces, raised or to be raised, for the defence of American liberty."

George Washington was a unanimous choice for the post. He was a fine selection for a variety of reasons. A wealthy aristocrat, his appointment would influence others of his class to support the Congress. A southerner, he would solicit greater devotion from that sector. He was no radical, and that would calm the fears of conservatives that this revolution was merely the work of wild and undisciplined minds and passions.

At forty-four, Washington was a tall, strong man of inspiring tranquillity and integrity, with an inner power that made other men confident; he possessed unlimited physical courage, sound judgment and self-control, and a character respected by everyone. But please others as he might, Washington held deep doubts about himself. He said:

" 'Tho I am truly sensible of the high Honour done me, in this Appointment, yet I feel great distress, from a consciousness that my abilities and military experience may not be equal to the extensive and important Trust: However, as the Congress desire it, I will enter upon the momentous duty,

Retreat of the British from Concord.

and exert every power I possess in their service, and for the support of the glorious cause. I beg they will accept my most cordial thanks for this distinguished testimony of their approbation."

And later, to Patrick Henry, Washington said emotionally: "Remember, what I now tell you. From the day I enter upon the command of the American armies I date my fall and the ruin of my reputation."

The Congress went on to choose other high-ranking officers, to provide for a coast guard, a marine force, and a navy. It urged the colonies to make allies of the Indians; and commissioners of Indian affairs were named. Supplies and munitions were to be collected, and where possible their manufacture begun. A hospital was organized for the army; and a post office was placed under the supervision of Benjamin Franklin.

Later, a so-called Olive Branch Petition was drawn up, aimed at achieving compromise with England, not war. In no way did it place blame for what had occurred on the King. It was careful not to advocate revolution, emphasizing colonial desire to remain within the British Empire, asking only for a modification of grievances. Congress also attempted to justify the actions taken by the colonists in "A Declaration setting forth the Causes and Necessity of their Taking up Arms." No mention was made of independence, though it maintained that "Our Cause is just. Our union is perfect . . . and with our (one) mind resolved to dye Freemen rather than live Slaves."

George III treated the Olive Branch Petition with royal scorn and declared the colonies to be in a state of rebellion, to be dealt with accordingly. England intended to suppress the colonials by force of arms. Benjamin Franklin, corresponding with a friend in Parliament, warned him against such a move: "If you flatter yourselves with beating us into submission, you know neither the people nor the country."

Events should have made this clear to the English earlier, but they appeared blind to what was happening, and why. On May 10, the same day the Second Continental Congress convened, a band of Green Mountain Boys, Vermonters under command of Ethan Allen, marched to Lake Champlain, attacked Fort Ticonderoga, and took it. Two days later, Allen captured Crown Point.

There was more. For the remainder of that month and into June, General Gage's army was bottled up in Boston, besieged by the colonial militia. On June 16, the Americans established themselves on Breed's Hill, alongside Bunker Hill in Charlestown, overlooking Boston. Aware that, unless he dislodged them, the city would become untenable, Gage decided to act.

He sent his men marching up the hill the next day in close battle order to the blaring of fifes and the beating of drums. A withering volley drove them back. They re-formed and returned, the colonists waiting until they could see "the whites' of their Eyes" before firing. Once again the redcoats were forced back. But they were stubborn and courageous, and they attacked again and finally won out when the Yankees ran out of ammunition. It was a costly victory. More than a thousand Englishmen died that day. Despite this triumph, the siege of Boston continued.

George Washington arrived in Cambridge at the beginning of July to take command of the army. Waiting for him was an untrained collection of men and boys, some sixteen thousand of them, mostly from Massachusetts, lacking discipline and uniforms. Their officers were elected, but without guarantees that their orders would be obeyed. Washington's problem was to mold these men into a competent fighting force. He set to work.

George III took similar action. It was vital to bolster his army, and he began negotiating for twenty thousand Russian mercenaries to help subdue the rambunctious colonists. The Czarina failed to appreciate the idea of her subjects dying for another ruler and rejected the offer. King George had to settle for Hessian fighting men.

In America, the issue was still being debated. Conservatives wanted to maintain colonial ties with England, to repair the breach against talk of independence. Others opposed them. One of the most persuasive voices was that of Thomas Paine. An Englishman, he had come to America in 1774, a man who had failed in almost every endeavor he had attempted. But he had captured the interest of Benjamin Franklin, who thought he might do well as a "clerk, or assistant tutor in a school, or assistant surveyor." Paine found work in Philadelphia with a printer and was soon editing the *Pennsylvania Magazine*. He was energetic in his support of the colonial cause.

In January 1776, his pamphlet called *Common Sense* was published. It was a demand for independence. Paine closed with a plea for an end to bickering, for unity, for support for the "Rights of Mankind and of the Free and Independent States of America . . . Every thing that is right or reasonable pleads for separation. The blood of the slain, the weeping voice of nature cries, 'TIS TIME TO PART."

Common Sense had a profound affect on the colonists, moving them toward unanimity as had nothing else, a giant step toward independence. There were others. The Provincial Congress of North Carolina declared for "Independency."

And Rhode Island's assembly authorized its delegates to take part in talks that would promote "the strictest union and confederation" among the colonies.

In Massachusetts, town meetings voted overwhelmingly to support independence.

Virginia also decided that its delegates should stand for independence. Richard Henry Lee, member of a prominent family, his sons at school in England, his brother an official in London, his income coming from the sale of tobacco to England, risked all when he submitted the following resolution to the Congress:

That these United Colonies are, and of right ought to be, free and independent states, that they are absolved from all allegiance to the British Crown, and that all political connection between them and the State of Great Britain is, and ought to be, totally dissolved; that it is expedient forthwith to take the most effectual measures for forming foreign Alliances; and that a plan of confederation be prepared, and transmitted to the respective colonies for their consideration and approbation.

John Adams promptly seconded the motion.

A heated debate followed. Much of the hostility stemmed from the belief that Congress had no authority to propose independence. The delegates, it was claimed, had not been commissioned by their individual colonies to separate them from England. Some delegates threatened to walk out of the Congress. Such men as Rutledge of South Carolina, Livingston of New York, Wilson of Pennsylvania, known as "king's men" and "royalists," argued against the resolution. John and Sam Adams fought for it, as did George

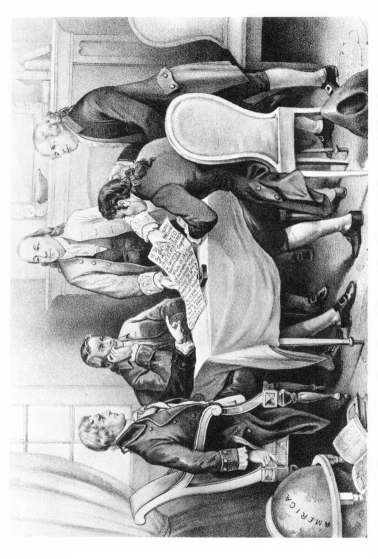

The Declaration Committee, left to right: Thomas Jefferson of Virginia, Roger Sherman of Connecticut, Benjamin Franklin of Pennsylvania, Robert R. Livingston of New York, and John Adams of Massachusetts.

Wythe of Virginia. It was suggested that action be postponed, both sides hoping to win over the others. The time was allowed.

Meanwhile, a committee was appointed, composed of Roger Sherman, Thomas Jefferson, Robert Livingston, Benjamin Franklin, and John Adams, to prepare a declaration of independence based on the Lee resolution.

Adams and Jefferson were selected by the other committeemen to produce a draft of the desired declaration. Adams was convinced that only Jefferson was suitably equipped for the task. Though only thirty-three years old, the tall Virginian was already highly regarded by his contemporaries. A student of the law, he had become a leader of the patriotic faction in the House of Burgesses. He had also helped to create Virginia's Committee of Correspondence, and his writing in its behalf was brilliant and logically reasoned. His reputation as a writer of addresses and resolutions had spread throughout the colonies, and Adams' faith in him was well grounded.

Jefferson set to work. He wrote on a portable desk placed across his knees, a desk of his own design, in the parlor of his apartment on the second floor of a house at Seventh and Market streets. He wrote swiftly, trying to reflect the feelings of his fellow Americans as they had been expressed over the years. He wanted to do two things: First, to declare for independence, stating clearly the reasons for such a radical move; Second, to advance the philosophy to which most of the colonists subscribed, and which had motivated them to act.

8

On July 1, in the Continental Congress, debate on the controversial Lee resolution was resumed. There was still no consensus. Pennsylvania opposed the resolution by a four to three vote, John Dickinson leading the opposition. He was anxious to make no move that would further anger England, unless France was committed to helping the colonies, and even that was not totally reassuring to him.

He said, "If we, by our Declaration of Independence, have bound ourselves to a war with Britain, what does France have to do but sit back and intimidate Britain until

Canada is put back in her hands. Then she can sit back and intimidate us."

The delegates stirred uneasily at that, none more than John Adams, who perceived the uncertainty in many of his fellow New Englanders. No new arguments were being made, but the old ones were no less effective for that. The delegates still were divided. Without unity, the resolution would be meaningless. And John Dickinson continued on his persuasive path against independence.

"I say: the time is not yet ripe for proclaiming it. Instead of help from foreign powers it will bring us disaster. I say: we ought to hold back any declaration and remain masters of our fate and fame. I say: we should keep Great Britain believing that we mean reconciliation. The whole nation is armed against us—the wealth of the empire is poured into her treasury—we shall weep at our folly!"

John Adams, at forty-one burly and short, weary but committed, stood to reply. He summarized all his previous arguments, answered all objections, concluded finally in a voice ringing with conviction and emotion: "For myself, I can only say this. I have crossed the Rubicon. All that I have, all that I am, all that I hope for in this life, I stake on our cause. For me, the die is cast. Sink or swim, live or die, to survive or perish with my country, that is my unalterable resolution!"

A vote was called. Nine colonies favored the resolution. South Carolina and Pennsylvania were against and New York abstained. Delaware's delegates were divided. It was decided to wait one more day.

Men searched their consciences anew, and some had second thoughts. John Dickinson realized that he could not honestly vote for independence, though convinced it was what the majority wanted. But he counted himself no less a patriot than any other man. After considering the matter in his reserved and quiet way, he donned his uniform as a colonel in Philadelphia's 1st Regiment. He would not return to the Congress. Instead, he rode off to New York to help General Washington in the defense of that city.

That same afternoon, South Carolina's delegates decided to vote for the resolution.

A rider was dispatched to ask Caesar Rodney, at his farm in Delaware, why he was not at the Congress. Rodney, the organizer of his colony's minutemen, was a certain vote for independence. When he learned that his might be the decisive vote, Rodney saddled his swiftest horse and galloped through a storm-drenched night for Philadelphia.

The next day the resolution was passed, only New York abstaining. A week later, she too approved.

Passage of the Lee resolution meant that the colonies had severed the political bonds which had tied them to England. Now there was the matter of the declaration Jefferson had prepared. John Adams studied it and suggested some minor alterations. They were made. Jefferson submitted it to Franklin. He too made some small changes. All that remained was submission to the Congress. By now it was late in the afternoon, hot and humid, and horseflies tormented the delegates in the white-paneled room of the State House. A resolution was offered and passed unanimously.

That this Congress will, tomorrow, again resolve itself into a committee of the whole, to take into their farther consideration the declaration of independence.

By the next morning, a lowering sense of urgency, if not doom, enveloped the delegates: They had learned that in

New York Washington's hastily assembled army was outnumbered by a force nearly twice its size. If Manhattan Island fell, then surely Philadelphia would be next, and all the talk and hopes and dreams would have been for nothing. The dispatches from New York were not encouraging:

"There remains no doubt of the whole of the [English] fleet from Halifax being now here. . . . They have landed under cover of their ships and have taken possession of Staten Island, from which in all probability they will soon make a descent upon us . . ."

Washington wanted more men, more supplies; and Benedict Arnold needed carpenters and shipbuilders at Crown Point. There were bills due and . . .

The morning expired slowly. It was past one o'clock when the Congress resolved itself into a Committee of the Whole, under the chairmanship of Benjamin Harrison. He read the title of the paper in his hand: "A Declaration of the Representatives of the United States of America in Congress Assembled . . ." It was the first time the words "United States of America" had been used to represent the thirteen colonies.

Harrison handed the document to the secretary, Mr. Thomson, a former teacher of Greek and Latin, a man with a fine speaking voice. He stood and began to read.

"When in the course of human events, it becomes necessary for one people to dissolve the bands which have connected them with another, and to assume among the powers of the earth, the separate and equal station to which the laws of nature and of nature's God entitle them, a decent respect to the opinions of mankind requires that they should declare the reasons which impel them to the separation. . . ."

The Declaration of Independence was not intended as a radical document. It was not created to foretell the future.

It was Jefferson's aim to offer "an expression of the American mind."

The Declaration had three parts. First, the Lee resolution. Second, the preamble. Here Jefferson had reached into the thinking of John Locke, an English political philosopher of a century earlier, borrowing heavily to justify what Americans were about to do. The crux of the argument was that "all men are created equal, that they are endowed by their Creator with certain unalienable Rights, that among these are Life, Liberty and the pursuit of Happiness." A similar article had been incorporated into the Virginia Bill of Rights. The declaration went on to say that "whenever any Form of Government becomes destructive of these ends, it is the right of the people to alter or to abolish it, and to institute new Government. . . ." In this fashion, the attempt was made to lay a legal and a moral foundation for the Revolution.

The final portion of the Declaration was a roster of twenty-eight grievances indicting George III. The truth or falsity of some of these was open to question, but on the whole this list of "facts" served its purpose, namely to unite the colonies. Later, Jefferson would say of the Declaration that he had not intended in it ". . . to find new principles, or new arguments, never thought of, not merely to say things which had never been said before; but to place before mankind the common sense of the subject, in terms so plain and firm as to command their assent . . . All its authority rests then on harmonizing sentiments of the day, whether expressed in conversation, in letters, printed essays, or the elementary books of public rights, as Aristotle, Cicero, Locke, Sidney . . ."

Finally, the secretary read the last of Jefferson's grievances, an indictment of George III's acquiescence to the slave trade. "Cruel war against human nature itself, violating the most sacred rights of life and liberty . . . captivating and carrying them into slavery in another hemisphere . . . the opprobrium of *infidel* powers, is the warfare of the *Christian* king of Great Britain, determined to keep open a market where MEN should be bought and sold . . . this execrable commerce . . ."

The reading of the Declaration ended. The debate began. And the issue of slavery took primacy over all others. The threat of Negro uprisings, financed and armed by the British, came under consideration.

"Should the English land troops in Georgia, twenty thousand Negroes at least would flock to their cause."

Edward Rutledge disagreed. "The King's friends have large plantations and property in slaves. If an uprising took place, they would lose these. And they cannot afford to risk it. That is our security."

"Slavery should be abolished," another delegate said. "It is wrong and immoral."

"The wisdom of slavery should be determined by the states themselves," Rutledge responded.

Another delegate said: "If left to itself in Georgia, it will be gradually ended. Let us not intermeddle. For the time being we cannot do without slave labor. Our whole economy would be ruined."

John Adams rose. "The whole thing is inconsistent with our principles," he said coldly.

The debate continued and finally Rutledge said: "The whole passage will have to be cut. If it stay, South Carolina can never agree to the Declaration."

The delegation from Georgia announced it was taking the same position.

The men in that hot chamber shifted unhappily. This

issue could sunder their ranks, shatter their resolve, end their hopes for freedom. There could be no doubt that they had arrived at an impasse. Those inclined toward slavery would not be moved, holding that one-sixth of the population should remain in bondage. The debate continued into the next day, July 4, until finally the men from South Carolina and Georgia had their way. The clause condemning slavery was struck from the document which declared all men to be equal.

Of this, Jefferson remarked: "The sentiments of men are known not only by what they receive but also by what they reject."

And later he wrote:

What a stupendous, what an incomprehensible machine is man! He can endure toil, famine, stripes, imprisonment and death itself in vindication of his own liberty—and the next moment be deaf to all those motives whose power supported him through his trial, and inflict on his fellow men a bondage . . . which he rose in rebellion to oppose!

So changes were made. And the final draft was read to the assembly, still a daring and powerful statement of human rights.

"We hold these truths to be self-evident, that all men are created equal, that they are endowed by their Creator with Certain unalienable Rights, that among these are Life, Liberty and the pursuit of Happiness,—That to secure these rights, Governments are instituted among Men, deriving their just Powers from the consent of the governed,—That whenever any Form of Government becomes destructive of these ends, it is the Right of the People to alter or to abolish it, and to institute new Government, laying its foundation on such principles and organizing its Powers in such form, as to them shall seem most likely to effect their Safety and Happiness. . . . But when a long train of abuses and usurpations, pursuing invariably the same Object evinces a design to reduce them under absolute Despotism, it is their right, it is their duty, to throw off such Government, and to provide new Guards for their future security."

And, the list of grievances, those restrictions and acts and impositions no longer to be tolerated. The Declaration closed with these words:

"And for the support of this Declaration, with a firm reliance on the Protection of divine Providence, we mutually pledge to each other our Lives, our Fortunes and our sacred Honor."

Now each member of the Congress had to vote. The roll, by states, for such they now were, was called. Josiah Bartlett, from New Hampshire, was first and the Georgian, Button Gwinnett, was the last. Each man declared himself in the best voice he could muster, this being no ordinary moment. At last it was over and the votes were tallied.

John Hancock announced the result. "The declaration by the representatives of the United States of America has been adopted unanimously."

A thick, anticipatory silence filled the chamber in the State House. And with good reason. The time to sign the Declaration had come. Once done, each of them would be marked traitor by his own hand. No man present failed to realize what lay ahead should the Revolution fail. Their homes, businesses, farms, all confiscated or destroyed, their families ruined, scattered, their good names blackened; and

Signing of the Declaration of Independence, July 4, 1776.

the royal gallows awaited them all. Such was the gravity of the situation that the names of the fifty-five men who signed that day were kept secret; fifteen others, not present, and those subsequently elected to the Congress added their signatures on August 2.

An entry in the "Secret Journal" read:

To prevent traitors and spies from worming themselves amongst us, no person shall have a seat in Congress until he should have signed the Declaration.

Yet no delegate hesitated for long. John Hancock, a reward of five hundred pounds on his head, stepped forward and inscribed his name with a bold flourish.

"There," he said. "His Majesty can now read my name without glasses. And he can double the reward on my head!"

They came in succession. Josiah Bartlett, William Whipple, Samuel Adams, John Adams, Roger Sherman, Stephen Hopkins, the latter hobbling to the dais with a cane, hand shaking. He said: "My hands may tremble but my heart does not!" And Francis Lewis, Lewis Morris, Abraham Clark, Caesar Rodney, Robert Morris, and Benjamin Franklin, who, before signing, spoke in a mild manner, "Indeed we must all hang together. Otherwise we shall most assuredly hang separately." Benjamin Rush, John Morton, William Paca, Thomas Jefferson, Carter Braxton, William Hooper, and Joseph Hewes, who was heard to murmur, "I have furnished myself with a good musket and bayonet. When I'm no longer useful in council I hope I shall be ready to take the field." There were others, men of varying sentiments about many matters, men whose minds were crowded and unsettled with doubts and fears, men of hope, acting in the spirit of rebellion, committing high treason and aware of the penalty, intent nevertheless on creating a new nation, daring to put their names to a document of defiance and faith.

The United States of America!

9

The Declaration of Independence altered the situation. Now the struggle was aimed at ending all political ties with England, at forming a new and independent state. Copies of the Declaration were made up as broadsides by printer John Dunlap and sent to the state assemblies, to all churches, to the officers of the militia, to the commander-in-chief of the Continental Army, to be proclaimed publicly.

The news spread throughout the former colonies, to each town and hamlet. In Philadelphia, bells were rung in celebration and there was great jubilation. In Boston, people cheered and fired their muskets and there was a slow,

measured cannon salute. In Connecticut, amid the cele-
brants, Matthew McHugh was jailed for speaking against
the Declaration. There were parades and speeches and
toasts. Flags were made and raised, and men enlisted for
the war.

The Declaration arrived in England, finally coming to
George III. The King expressed his sentiments to Parliament. "One great advantage will be derived . . . of the rebels
being openly avowed. We shall have unanimity at home
founded in the general conviction of the justice and necessity of our measures."

So word of the Declaration, and its radical and wonder-
ful meaning, spread and was translated into the various
languages of the world. In France men listened, and haughty
aristocrats understood that what had happened might affect
even them; and it was the same in Africa, in Asia, in Germany, Russia, Italy. . . .

In New York City, where hundreds of British warships
rode at anchor in the harbor or on the horizon, each crowded
with trained veteran troops, where Staten Island was already an English stronghold, the reading of the Declaration
occasioned noisy salutes which burned up sorely needed
gunpowder. A gilded statue of George III mounted on
horseback was toppled from its perch.

George Washington disapproved of such activities, but
he had more urgent matters on his mind. A glance out to
sea reminded him of the great odds which faced him and
his men. Further, there was a shortage of supplies, and all
his requests to Congress had availed him little. Each day
brought to his attention evidence of venality and selfishness
that moved him to despair. He wrote:

Such a dearth of public spirit, such want of virtue,

such stockjobbing and such fertility in all the low arts to obtain advantages of one kind or another, I never saw before, and pray God's mercy that I may never be witness to again.

There were many Americans who owned a minimum of enthusiasm for prosecuting a war for independence. These Tories, mostly property holders, were anxious to continue the attachment to England and so protect their businesses and other financial interests. Many of them were motivated by the sincere belief that the brightest future for America would come out of a colonial condition. These Loyalists—about one-third of the population—included the military, many members of the Anglican Church, and most officeholders. Even Washington had been privately opposed to the concept of independence as late as 1775, although, like so many others, he changed his mind by the middle of the following year.

Troubled about the course the Revolution might take, aware that political conflagrations often get out of control, are frequently betrayed, some 60,000 Loyalists chose to leave America. Of those who stayed, some transferred their property to relatives or friends who were looked upon favorably by the revolutionists, hoping to wait out the trouble at a minimum cost to themselves and their families. Only about one-third of all Americans took any active role in the Revolution. On the other hand, many conservatives, who had fought long and hard against independence, who were opposed on principle to rebellion, now took up arms in the American cause.

Radicals came from all levels of life. There were merchants and small farmers, craftsmen and ne'er-do-wells, shopkeepers and aristocratic planters. Few among them considered that they were making a social as well as a political revolution; they were intent on protecting their property, the rights of gentlemen, the status and privileges of the upper classes. Only a very few of them recognized the true nature of their fellow Americans, their restless spirit, the rejection of inhibiting strictures of any kind, the deep-seated desire of each to better himself.

But the time for introspection was not now. There was a war to be fought and to this purpose propagandists on both sides of the Atlantic were busy disseminating one point of view or the other, their words only partly directed at domestic ears. Their targets were the nations of Europe in general, Spain and France in particular. And with good reason. These were the two nations most likely to join in the fray; both would be overjoyed to do England any damage. Neither government, however, was anxious to take unnecessary risks, so their representatives listened and observed, but did little.

The Revolution offered military problems to both sides, problems that made the outcome uncertain. England was the most powerful and the wealthiest nation on earth, its population about twelve million people. By contrast, the Americans had little money, and there were less than three million of them, and not too many of these were anxious to fight.

Early in 1776, Washington commanded only about 18,-000 men, the peak enlistment of the war. When the fighting finally ceased, there were less than 5,000 soldiers in uniform. Few Americans enjoyed serving in the Army and would give only a few months of their time at most, leaving as soon as conditions became unsuitable. By necessity then, the Revolution became a militiaman's war, small groups fighting under local leaders, whenever it suited them to do so. Once a region was made safe from the English, they returned to more peaceful pursuits.

Yet the English were unable to take much advantage of the situation. For if there were Americans with strong English leanings, there were also many Englishmen sympathetic to America, and George III found it exceedingly difficult to raise an army, one of the reasons he employed Hessian troops.

At the time fighting broke out, there were some 9,000 redcoats in and around Boston, but they were pinned down. Americans controlled the entire coastline, an impressive advantage. Pacifying the former colonials was going to be a formidable task. The British had to work their way inland, foot by foot, fighting all along the way against an enemy that was able to strike quickly in small, highly mobile bands, able to inflict casualties and scatter before a counterattack could be launched, a kind of warfare learned from the Indians.

To the British Army, this meant lengthening vulnerable supply lines and large casualty lists. Complicating the matter was the fact of a battlefield three thousand miles from the homeland, one familiar in every way to the enemy. Helping to cancel out this advantage was England's highly developed industry, capable of supplying all her war needs. The United States had no industry worth mentioning.

Despite this, colonial leaders proceeded with a high degree of optimism. And with reason. This was indeed a people's rebellion and as such the British stood little chance of achieving a clear-cut victory. Not even a great military triumph could provide that, for there was no way of preventing guerrilla warfare, the sniping, raiding, and ambushes allowing the redcoats no rest, no time to consolidate their positions. On the other hand, such forays alone would never provide total victory for America.

Important military activities actually commenced before the signing of the Declaration of Independence. In the autumn of 1775, an American expedition penetrated into Canada, its aim to win Canadians over to the revolutionary cause and achieve a dramatic military victory. On the last day of the year, generals Benedict Arnold and Richard Montgomery led an attack on the city of Quebec. It was a desperate scheme and might have caused irretrievable harm to the hopes of the young nation.

Arnold personally led 650 men into the city, where he was greeted by a deadly defense. Many of his men were wounded, and he took a musket ball in the leg. About 100 Americans, including General Montgomery, died in the battle, and 400 others were captured. The British lost only five men.

The English dispatched a fleet and an army to deal with the invaders and a retreat was ordered. It began in May 1776 and lasted into July, with over 5,000 casualties. The disastrous nature of the campaign ended America's Canadian ambitions, and left the United States vulnerable to invasion. The British were more concerned with defending Quebec and made no effort to strike south.

The news from Boston was better. The threat to the British troops in that city came from Dorchester Heights, which the Americans had occupied at night, establishing strong defenses. Unable to dislodge the "peasant" rebels, the English commander, Sir William Howe, decided to evacuate the city. In March, he loaded his army, and about 1,000 Tories, aboard 170 ships and sailed for Halifax.

Benedict Arnold.

With the fall of Boston, the British no longer controlled any portion of the country.

But Sir William was already plotting his next move. He was anxious to win control over the main coastal cities—New York and Philadelphia. In this way he could split the colonies and seriously weaken their efforts, rupture communications and sources of supplies. New York was the primary target. He intended to shut down that fine harbor, secure Manhattan Island, then use the Hudson River as a wedge to isolate New England from the other colonies.

In 1776, some 25,000 people lived in New York City, and many of them now set to work erecting fortifications against the anticipated British attack. At the same time, General Washington was arranging his forces strategically on the other islands in the harbor.

On July 2, the same day Howe was putting 10,000 troops onto Staten Island, the same day Lee's resolution was being voted on in Philadelphia, Washington went before his men to speak about the impending battle.

"The fate of unborn millions," he said solemnly, "will now depend, under God, on the courage and conduct of this army . . . Let us therefore animate and encourage each other, and show the whole world, that a free man contending for liberty on his own ground is superior to any slavish mercenary on earth."

Such lofty sentiments fell short of what was needed against an enemy daily growing stronger. British ships were able to sail with virtual immunity past Yankee guns at the Battery, at Red Hook, and on Governor's Island. Then Sir William was reinforced by his brother, Admiral Lord Richard Howe, with a large naval fleet. Additional reinforcements kept coming until the British Army numbered 32,000 men, including nine thousand Germans.

The Battle of Long Island.

Howe prepared thoroughly for the coming battle. He recalled too vividly Breed's Hill, where he had won, but at a terrible cost because of Yankee tactics. He meant to prevent that from happening again. Moreover, he was convinced that he could quickly put down this rebellion by enticing the Americans out of their entrenched positions, especially at Brooklyn Heights on Long Island. He intended to take Long Island before turning his attention to Manhattan itself.

On August 22, Howe began landing his troops on Long Island, and four days later, at dusk, attacked the entrenched colonials. The Americans were taken by surprise, the British advancing along unguarded roads, not identified till they were within fifty yards of the positions. The undisciplined Americans panicked, and officers lost control. The fighting became vicious as the opposing forces came to close quarters and used bayonets, the Americans taking heavy casualties.

Washington had been in personal command during this humiliating defeat and he recognized the desperateness of his situation. It was vital that he get his men off Long Island, regroup, and so be able to continue the battle at a time and a place more to his liking. On the night of August 29 a thick fog settled over the harbor, and Washington hurried to take advantage of it. To deceive the enemy, he ordered his men to leave their campfires burning, and move into waiting boats.

Once again nature came to Washington's aid. A strong northwest wind had kept the English warships from entering the East River, leaving that waterway open to him. When daylight came, Sir William Howe saw what had happened, but there was nothing he could do.

Now many members of the Continental Army began

to desert and Washington had no funds with which to tempt them to stay on. "The impulse for going home," he admitted, "was so irresistible it answered no purpose to oppose it." He went on to say that he was "left by the Troops just when they begin to deserve the name, or perhaps at a Moment when an important blow is expected."

Anxious to take New York, Howe searched for a weak spot in the island's defenses at which to make an invasion. He chose Kip's Bay. Here only a few inexperienced soldiers were on duty. At first sight of the redcoats, the Americans panicked. They dropped their muskets and ran. Howe's men came ashore without being forced to fire even a single shot. And that easily, New York belonged to the British.

10

Unable to launch a counterattack, Washington ordered his men north. He hoped to mount a better defense in the hills. In order to do so effectively, however, he needed information about the strength and plans of the enemy.

Captain Nathan Hale volunteered to go behind enemy lines and learn what he could. He was captured on Long Island and identified as an American officer. Brought to Manhattan, he was questioned by General Howe, who ordered him executed. There was no trial.

In October, Howe again tried to outflank Washington, but the Virginian anticipated the strategy and withdrew.

The ensuing Battle of White Plains took place on October 28, with inconclusive results. The Americans pulled back again, this time north of New Castle.

When the division, some 3,000 men, stationed at Fort Washington fell into British hands, General Cornwallis was able to transport his troops across the Hudson River, forcing General Nathanael Greene to evacuate Fort Lee.

Matters were progressing favorably for the British. General Howe found life among the best people in New York pleasurable and decided to remain in the city; he ordered Cornwallis to pursue the rebels.

This was a bleak period for Americans and hopes for the revolutionary cause were dim. Congress called for all patriots to stand firm and show courage. Nevertheless, with Philadelphia vulnerable to attack, the Congress fled to Lancaster, and then to York, an even more remote village, anxious to avoid capture.

Washington kept moving. From New Castle he went into New Jersey to join up with Greene, then back to comparatively secure positions in Pennsylvania. The weather turned cold and winter settled over the land. Howe ordered his troops back to New York to wait for spring.

At Trenton, 1,400 Hessians under Colonel Johann Rahl, confident of their ability to defeat the rebels, remained encamped behind inadequate defenses. Washington decided to attack. On Christmas night, he personally led his men across the Delaware River, advancing on the Hessian positions in the morning. It was a swift and stunning victory with only five American casualties. Nine hundred prisoners were taken.

Washington cast about for another victory to help shore up sagging colonial spirits. He also wanted to intimidate the British soldiers, to make them aware that they faced an

Washington crossing the Delaware.

enemy able to inflict considerable punishment. Leaving a token force at Trenton, he marched for Princeton, stealing past Cornwallis and his army. Princeton provided another triumph, and now Washington was able to set up camp at Morristown.

These setbacks caused little concern among the English generals. They were confident about the eventual outcome of the struggle. Howe planned carefully so that by the spring of 1777 he would be able to launch moves that would end the insurrection for all time. He expected a final victory before year's end. After all, he reasoned, Washington commanded only about 4,000 men, a very small threat, especially in light of the continuing buildup of English military strength in America.

The British battle plan was simple and traditionally sound—divide and conquer. Isolate the various colonies, cut them off from outside aid, subdue each in turn, and so terminate matters.

To this end, General John Burgoyne moved out of Canada with 7,700 men, by way of Lake Champlain. He intended to strike at Albany, even as Howe dispatched an expedition north from New York. Between them, they would trap the rebels in that area.

It seemed like a reasonable plan. First, Burgoyne hit hard at Ticonderoga, coming away with a decisive victory. And then, Albany.

But Howe had never actually approved of this scheme, preferring a strategy of his own. He hoped to split the colonies in two with one dramatic blow, ending the war abruptly, with a minimum of difficulty. He decided to act on his own.

He marched into Pennsylvania, proceeding on Philadelphia, expecting to smash Washington's army at the same time he took the City of Brotherly Love. Washington, however, had other ideas. He refused to be drawn into combat and eluded Howe's best efforts. It was a frustrated Sir William who eventually realized that he had failed in his dream of a quick triumph, and had lost his chance to join Burgoyne at Albany as well.

Burgoyne would have been grateful for any help. Rain had converted the roads of upper New York into strands of mud, slowing his advance to a virtual crawl. Horses and men, cannon and supply wagons slipped and slid, went into the ditches, caused delays, and the loss of valuable materiel. Nor was that all. As word of his coming flashed across the countryside, farmers and townspeople took down their muskets and prepared to resist. Each passing day saw the advantage shift toward the rebels until Burgoyne's army was outnumbered by some three to one.

Convinced that his only chance for success lay in a sudden aggressive move, Burgoyne ordered an attack. At Saratoga, the Americans hit back, and with devastating effect, 1,200 redcoats falling. Burgoyne was desperate. Expected help had failed to materialize and without it his army faced annihilation. Grim and bitter, he chose the least cruel of the choices left to him—he surrendered.

Saratoga was a key victory for America. For the first time it was evident that the Continental Army could meet the British head on and defeat them. Even more, it prevented the English from dividing the colonies. Saratoga also engaged the attention of various nations around the world, none more so than France.

In England there was considerable sentiment for conciliation. Should that happen, and England come out of the Revolution undefeated, it would have left the island empire still powerful and aggressive, her prestige relatively undamaged.

France craved revenge on Britain for past defeats and now the opportunity loomed in Saratoga. Louis XVI had already aided the American cause, having made one million *livres* available to the colonists two months before the Declaration of Independence, the money to be used to purchase munitions. This money, to a large degree, made it possible to prosecute the Revolution, since America was largely an agricultural nation and unable to manufacture the required military supplies.

Now more help was needed, overt military support. Congress dispatched to Paris the one man who seemed equal to the task—Benjamin Franklin. Then in his seventies, Franklin was welcomed grandly by the French, who quoted his witticisms and entertained him lavishly, appreciating his fine intelligence and infinite humanity. But they had made no effort to advance the aid he sought. Until Saratoga.

Exploiting the French fear of an American-English reconciliation, Franklin maneuvered Paris diplomats into signing two treaties, one of alliance, the other of amity and commerce. The former stated that it aimed to uphold the "liberty, sovereignty, and independence absolute and unlimited of the United States." Further, it renounced French claims to the Bermuda Islands and any portion of North America east of the Mississippi River. And, if the United States were to conquer Canada, or the Bermudas, France promised to affirm them as belonging to the new nation. In return, the United States would recognize any French acquisitions in the West Indies.

France tried to strengthen the alliance by enlisting Spain. But that nation owned many colonies and was reluctant to make common cause with a colonial independence movement. After all, who could predict where such a strange idea might lead? France and the United States also agreed that neither country would make a separate peace with England and that neither would cease fighting until independence was a fact.

However, any optimism generated in Paris had little effect on the soldiers of the Continental Army during the winter of 1777–78. To them the future seemed gloomy and filled with despair. Washington had chosen Valley Forge, in Pennsylvania, for his headquarters and here a combination of circumstances was to cause great hardship for the men. Though that winter was no colder than those of other years, it may have seemed worse to the ordinary soldier. There was faulty management of supplies and the required cold-weather gear, clothing, and blankets failed to reach the men.

Worse, there were Americans of every political hue who did business with the British, even as the Revolution continued, receiving gold in payment for their goods or services. The Continental Army could not compete. Washington could pay only in specie, paper money not thought to be worth much, and was considered a poor customer. Illness also weakened the ranks of the patriots. A shortage of food convinced many regulars not to renew their enlistments.

Finally recognizing the need for reform, Congress reorganized the commissary department and the quartermaster unit. And a new training program was instituted. Soon the men of the Continental Army began to resemble true soldiers. With the coming of spring, Washington knew that he commanded a force of toughened veterans.

For the British, occupying Philadelphia, that winter was much more pleasant. Life among the polite and agree-

Washington and Lafayette visiting the winter headquarters at Valley Forge.

able society of the city was enjoyable. There were parties and galas for the officers; and the men lived comfortably and were warm.

But spring brought back the harsh realities of war. Sir Henry Clinton relieved Howe, bringing with him orders to evacuate the city and move north in order to protect lines of communication out of New York City. At the same time, he intended to inhibit any French moves against Canada. Though Paris had yet to declare itself officially, it was no secret that the French had thrown in with America. A French fleet had already begun operating in American coastal waters, providing the naval power the rebels lacked.

The evacuation of Philadelphia took ten days, was completed on June 18. The next day Washington broke camp and started after the British column. All along the line of march, the English found themselves harried, sniped at; these hit-and-run tactics caused many casualties and a number of desertions.

That same month, France formally entered the fray. Spain continued to eye the proceedings with interest, anxious to deliver a blow at England, but still reluctant to support the new nation. Spain finally did enter the war in June of 1779, but made it clear that she was allied with France, not the United States. The Spanish intended to straddle the issue no matter how awkward the stance might be.

Now England was forced to battle on several fronts. Aware of the ambitions of her enemies on the European continent, she had to protect herself from possible invasion. American hopes for victory increased.

The British, however, were far from beaten. Sir Henry Clinton was a much more aggressive soldier than Howe had been. He recovered Georgia for England in 1779 and launched a war of attrition against the towns and cities to the north. Though no decisive battle was fought, there was considerable activity on all fronts.

Meanwhile, in New York, covert and devious matters were occurring. Benedict Arnold, patriot and soldier, a key figure in the capture of Ticonderoga, in the campaign against Canada, the battle of Valcour Island, the victory at Saratoga, began to feel that his efforts were not being fully appreciated, that other, less deserving, men were receiving promotions that should have come to him. And Congress had promoted five men, all his juniors, to higher rank. His young wife, Peggy, member of a Tory family, made no effort to soften his resentment.

Complicating Arnold's life was a rising tide of debt, brought on by his lavish mode of living. Adding to his dissatisfaction was the professional criticism which had been leveled at him. He contemplated ways of obtaining the military and economic rewards so important to him. Early in 1780, when General Washington reprimanded him for abuse of his authority, Arnold decided he had had enough; he renewed negotiations begun at an earlier time with the British. He contacted Sir Henry Clinton, suggesting that he could arrange to become commandant of the fortress at West Point, a strategic site overlooking the Hudson River. Once that was done, he would be in a position to supply the British with plans of the fortifications, making it easy for them to capture the post. An agreement was made.

Arnold made good his boast. He persuaded Washington to give him command of West Point. Once established, he arranged a meeting with Major John André, Clinton's adjutant and a friend of Mrs. Arnold, at Haverstraw. Arnold turned over the plans of the fortress, plus information about those defensive positions most vulnerable to attack.

The Capture of André.

André prepared to return to New York. A ship, the *Vulture,* had carried him upstream, but American fire had forced it to sail back down the Hudson. André had no choice but to return to his headquarters overland. Disregarding orders, he stripped off his army uniform and donned civilian clothing.

Near Tarrytown he was hailed by three armed Americans. Perhaps they saw the lone traveler as an easy mark to rob. They searched him and in one of his shoes discovered the plans to West Point. Convinced that they had stumbled onto something too important for them to deal with, they delivered André to their officer. He immediately identified the plans and, hoping to alert West Point to possible danger, sent word to General Arnold informing him of André's capture. Arnold promptly fled to New York City.

When Washington learned what had happened, he ordered West Point reinforced, the weak spots shored up. Major André was court-martialed, found guilty of spying, and hanged.

As for Benedict Arnold, he was commissioned a brigadier general in the British Army, rewarded with six thousand pounds in cash and a pension for his wife, plus either pensions or military commissions for his children. In his new role, he led two raids for the English, one against Virginia, the other against New London, Connecticut. When peace came, he went to England to live, but was never content there, being subjected to abuse and losing most of his fortune in bad investments. He died in 1801.

The Revolution went on. The French Navy, operating almost exclusively in the Caribbean, failed to become a major influence. British ships controlled virtually the entire eastern shoreline. American harbors were blockaded. Shipping was attacked with serious damage to the revolutionary cause. On land, English attacks on New Bedford, New Haven, New London, and Virginia extracted heavy costs.

Washington lacked the military strength to attack the British in New York, but he did send General Anthony Wayne against the fort at Stony Point; and he ordered Light Horse Harry Lee into action against Paulus Hook, now part of Jersey City.

Provisions were also made to defend the western frontiers. Both Pennsylvania and New York had been badly hurt by raids conducted by the Tories and their Indian allies of the Six Nations. John Sullivan, captured by the British during the battle for Long Island, and later exchanged, was commissioned to do something about the situation. He led 5,000 fighting men into the Chemung Valley and made contact with the enemy at Newtown, roundly defeating them and laying waste to much of the Iroquois country.

Goose Van Schaick headed another expedition against the Onondaga Indians and Daniel Brodhead defeated the Indians of Pennsylvania. George Rogers Clark operated against the tribes in the Ohio Valley, occupying a number of towns in the Illinois country, pacifying the frontiers.

Fighting and bloodshed were only part of the revolutionary struggle. A very small percentage of Americans was in the field at any one time, and some portions of the new nation, the interior of New England, for example, never saw a redcoat. Casualties on both sides were not especially heavy, yet no one in America remained untouched by the conflict.

War, as it traveled back and forth over the cities and the farms, took a heavy toll. Houses were wrecked, crops ruined, villages pillaged and looted—destruction was widespread. British soldiers, bitter and resentful, appropriated livestock, tobacco, and other crops, took slaves from plantations, fired barns and homes alike. Often patriot soldiers did likewise, either unable or unwilling to distinguish between friend and foe, caught up in the terror and hatred of the battle.

The war interrupted the ordinary lives and commerce of all the people. Trade was slowed, if not entirely halted, shipping made difficult, marketing often impossible. New England's fishermen were unable to cast their nets, fearful of British patrol boats.

Money was always a problem. In 1776, in an attempt to raise desperately needed money, Congress authorized a national lottery. Though four hundred thousand tickets were printed, the hoped-for income never fully materialized.

Among those private citizens who tried to ease the tight money situation was Haym Salomon. Polish-born, he had settled in New York in 1772, and established a successful brokerage house. After the revolution began, he was twice imprisoned by the British as a spy. At last he escaped to Philadelphia, where he assisted Robert Morris in obtaining loans from France and the Netherlands. In addition, he pledged his personal fortune. These large and unrepaid loans to the patriot cause brought about his postwar bankruptcy. He died at forty-five, his health ruined by his imprisonments. His heirs were left penniless.

There was little hard currency during the Revolution, neither gold nor silver. Each of the thirteen states, in addition to the Continental Congress, took to printing its own paper money. Anxious to prevent a ruinous inflation, Congress asked the individual states to stop printing money of their own, thus hoping to lend more value to the federal script. The states refused. The money presses continued to roll and by the close of 1779 two hundred million Continental dollars had been issued. In the summer of 1778, a gold dollar was worth four of the Continental variety; a year later the ratio was almost a hundred to one.

Inflation reached such heights in 1780 that in Boston beef sold for $10 a pound; butter was $12 a pound; corn went for $150 a bushel; and Samuel Adams reported on the purchase of a suit and a hat—the cost: $2,000.

For some Americans, inflation was a good thing. Farmers suffered not at all, food being in constant demand. And privateers made huge profits from their forays against British shipping. John and Andrew Cabot of Massachusetts were particularly successful, establishing a family fortune that has carried down to this day; also fortunate were the Derbys of Salem, and Stephen Higginson of the same village. Though privateering involved certain risks, the rewards were considerably better than those from fighting under General Washington.

Inflation hit hardest at the officers and men of the Continental Army. Their wages were low, and to make matters worse they were paid in Continental dollars so that they were hurt by rising prices as well as a diminishing currency. The enlisted men were fortunate: they received food and clothing. Officers had to provide both for themselves. To complicate matters, military payrolls were often months behind. Washington lamented: "The long and great sufferings of this army is unexampled in history."

The situation became so bad that one officer wrote: "I despise my countrymen. I wish I could say I was not born in America. I once gloried in it but am now ashamed of it."

The activities of the Tories on behalf of England was

a complicating factor. They were everywhere in great numbers, supplying the redcoats with food and shelter and issuing propaganda. They counterfeited Continental money in an effort to make it even more worthless, served as spies and guides, and led the Indians against vulnerable outposts. Some Tories fought with the British regulars, even forming their own military companies.

A popular definition of a loyalist was "a thing whose head is in England, whose body is in America, and its neck ought to be stretched."

Feelings ran high. Violence broke out from time to time against Tories, and there was considerable sentiment for restrictive legislation. As far back as January 1776, Congress recommended Tory rights of free speech be curtailed, allowing none of them to write or speak against America. Further, it was urged that the separate states seize Tory property and sell it, lending the monies received to the federal government.

That was all the encouragement the states needed. Laws were made and enforced repressing Tories. An oath of allegiance was required of them, and those who refused to take it were deprived of their citizenship. They lost the right to vote. They were denied access to the courts and in some places were prevented from practicing law. Fines and special taxes were levied against them. Many were confined to their homes or moved from them arbitrarily. In some states, Tories were not allowed to become teachers. Charges of treason were leveled, and the death penalty, though seldom imposed, threatened all loyalists.

Confiscation of property was the primary and most telling punishment, especially when coupled with banishment, legal or otherwise. Thousands of Tories were forced to flee, and eventually about 100,000 became exiles, either through banishment or because they refused to live under the revolutionary order. When hostilities ended, some Tories came home, and, for the most part, were permitted to live in peace.

11

Nationalism in America was the result of the Revolution rather than the cause of it. To be sure, prior to the outbreak of fighting, there were common areas among the colonies—language, tradition, religion. There was even a sense of pride in being an American. But the yearning to form a new nation had not yet been in evidence; that came only out of a succession of events, commencing with passage of the Stamp Act. In time the feeling for union grew stronger, though suspicion of a powerful central government remained.

But it was the Continental Congress on behalf of the

united states which prosecuted the war against England, which made an alliance with France, and which eventually made peace. Clearly, the phrase, United Colonies, and later, United States, owned a singular as well as a plural meaning.

Before the Declaration of Independence was proclaimed, it became apparent that a strong central government was needed. The Second Continental Congress lacked the flexibility, authority, and strength necessary to administer the complex problems a new nation was bound to encounter. Obviously a body of law was called for to define and limit the new government. Anything less would result in confusion and chaos.

As early as June 7, 1776, a clause in the Lee resolution proposed that a "plan of confederation be prepared and transmitted to the respective Colonies for their consideration and approbation."

Four days later a committee, under John Dickinson, was named to draft such a document. But, in the usual manner of such bodies, the committee moved sluggishly and independence had already been declared by the time they finally reported.

The committee proposed a formalization of the situation then in effect, with Congress assuming all the responsibilities and functions of a central government, its delegates to be appointed on a yearly basis by the states. Some affairs were to remain in the hands of the states, others relegated to Congress. The committee did not suggest how decisions were to be enforced.

In time the members of Congress came to consider and debate the Dickinson report. They soon discovered that few of them were equipped by experience or inclination to deal with the difficulties involved in running a country. Even more, they learned that most Americans suspected

Congress even as they had suspected imperial governors, the Parliament, the King himself.

This attitude was summed up by young Edward Rutledge of South Carolina when he wrote:

> I am resolved to vest the Congress with no more power than is absolutely necessary, and to use a familiar expression, to keep the staff in our own hands.

Rutledge was not alone. Others in Congress also viewed all government with distrust. Dr. Thomas Burke, a delegate from North Carolina, was such a man. He considered himself a guardian of local interests, his concern with the larger enterprise at a minimum. Burke led a swelling chorus of dissent whenever there was movement toward establishing workable governmental institutions.

"We are met to protect the interests of the people," Burke declaimed. "To exclude those tyrannies which would enslave our peoples, to gain our freedom from England, not to substitute one ultimate authority with another."

A delegate responded. "To gain freedom and maintain it we must create a government firm enough to win the war."

"This Congress," Burke replied, "is all the government necessary to that end and I would favor dissolving even this body once the struggle is triumphantly concluded."

An uneasy murmur filled the chamber. This sort of talk presaged no good for the future of the young country. Another delegate rose to speak.

"You suggest anarchy, sir. These United States of—"

"Independent states," Burke interrupted hotly. "Thirteen sovereign states, I remind you, sir, each responsible to itself in public and private affairs—"

"National sentiment runs too strong to allow serious

consideration of your proposal, Dr. Burke, that we dissolve the Congress. More, we must form a stable Federal structure, one that will rule wisely and profitably."

Burke snorted contemptuously. "In such suggestions I perceive the grasping for power that signals the degeneration into tyranny. I for one will entertain no risk of erecting a new evil to replace the old."

The debate continued and Burke's point of view gained adherents. His arguments did nothing to elevate popular sentiment in favor of a national government. Esteem for state goverments was on the rise. The best efforts of the Congress to run the country, to win the war, to establish law and order, to create institutions where there were none, to provide discipline and direction were received with little enthusiasm. This was particularly true when it came to money. The states, able to levy taxes, attained a degree of solvency. The national government, lacking this authority, sank deeper into an economic swamp as a result of its deluge of near worthless paper.

One of the most divisive problems facing the nation was the disposition of the western territories reserved for the Indians. A bitter debate raged over it and postponed consideration of a new constitution. Six states—Delaware, Maryland, New Jersey, Rhode Island, Pennsylvania, and New Hampshire—with no claims on that unsettled land wanted to limit the western boundaries of those states which did make such claims, fearful of the power expansion would provide.

Five of the states based their claims on royal charters which gave them sea-to-sea control. Virginia maintained that not only did it have authority over all lands sea-to-sea but over the territory north of the Ohio River, and the Kentucky River. It became evident that a government more powerful than the Continental Congress would be required to settle this dispute.

Gradually this view took hold and more consideration was given to the Dickinson report. But many areas of controversy existed and had to be worked out. One such was the amount of representation each state would have in a central legislature. This was finally resolved in favor of one vote for each state, no matter how large the territory or population.

And there was the problem of money. From where would come the funds necessary to operate a national government? Congress was about to discover that it was much easier to translate patriotism into blood and death than into dollars and cents. Finally it was agreed that all expenses would be shared among the states according to "the value of all land within each state. . . ."

The continuing conflict over the western lands was further complicated by the selfish interests of land speculators, such as the Indiana and Illinois-Wabash companies. They labored covertly and openly for cession of the territories to the federal government, hoping then to be able to claim them for their own profits. But the landed states, backed in Congress by local speculators, prevailed, and a motion was passed which declared that "no state shall be deprived of territory for the benefit of the United States."

Parochial interests and provincial attitudes postponed the solution of vital problems. Loyalty to a particular colony rather than to the whole nation was a habit difficult to break.

A New Jersey man said of Virginians that their ownership of large plantations "blows up the owners to an imagination . . . that they are exalted as much above other Men in worth & precedency, as . . . in their property." A visitor from Massachusetts wrote that South Carolinians were addicted to "cards, dice, the bottle and horses," practiced widespread desecration of the Sabbath, possessed an "odious character." Lewis Morris of New York stipulated in his will that he wanted his son to avoid an education in Connecticut "lest he should imbibe in his youth that lowe craft and cunning so incident to the People of that Colony."

And shortly after the Declaration of Independence had been promulgated, George Washington issued a general order denouncing the "jealousies &c" that had come into being among the soldiers from various sections, warning his men to ignore "distinctions of Nations, Countries, and Provinces" and collectively to assume the mantle of Americanism.

These differences of opinion served only to weaken the nation when the need for unity was greatest. Yet concepts of union were nothing new on the continent: there had been the New England Confederation and the Albany Plan of Union; and in 1775 Benjamin Franklin had suggested to the Continental Congress that a United Colonies of North America be formed for friendship and the common defense. Americans recognized the need for union, though at the same time remaining fearful of it. They were anxious to further the self-interest of this state or that section, wary of a great and centralized authority.

It was clear, however, that the former colonies could not split off in different directions, not if independence were to be protected and strengthened. Prejudices and honest differences alike had to be put aside. A union strong enough to prosecute the rebellion to a successful conclusion had to be formed.

So it was that out of John Dickinson's committee came a draft of the Articles of Confederation, as the document was called. After several revisions, after fussing and debat-

John Dickinson.

ing, after tinkering with this clause and that word, the first constitution of the United States, with a preamble and 13 articles, was approved by Congress on November 15, 1777. Article I stated, "The style of this confederacy shall be The United States of America."

The Articles delegated to the central government—Congress was its sole department—an imposing roster of powers. Congress took to itself exclusive authority over relations with all foreign countries, to include the making of war and peace, the disposition of admiralty cases, disputes between the states, the establishment of weights and measures, trade with the Indians beyond the borders of the states, postal services, and the coining of money. Congress also reserved the right to requisition the states for men and money and to contract loans. Decisions were to be reached by a simple majority, each state having a single vote, except in certain important matters on which the approval of nine states would be necessary.

Perhaps most important, the Articles left to the states the power of the purse. Congress could requisition funds but it had no effective method of enforcing the demand. The Articles protected the states against each other; the principle of one vote for one state guaranteed the rights of the smaller states, and a nine-state majority served to shield the larger from collusion by a group of the less powerful.

All that remained was for the individual states to approve the Articles to make the document the law of the land. Copies went out from Congress with an accompanying letter, a letter almost apologetic in tone:

Hardly is it to be expected that any plan . . . should exactly correspond with the maxims and political views of every particular State . . . This is proposed as the best which could be adapted to the circumstances of all; and as that alone which affords any tolerable prospect of a general ratification . . . It will confound our foreign enemies, defeat the flagitious practices of the disaffected, strengthen and confirm our friends, support our public credit, restore the value of our money, enable us to maintain our fleets and armies, and add weight and respect to our councils at home, and to our treaties abroad. In short, this salutary measure can no longer be deferred.

Conditioned by experience to observe all government with a jaundiced eye, Americans found it difficult to ratify the Articles.

Town meetings were held. Each article was dissected and exposed; defects were pointed out and dangers to men and property loudly noted. In state legislatures, representatives fought for their particular viewpoints, determined to limit as much as possible the power of Congress.

The further weakening of the already soft provisions of the Articles posed a serious threat which was recognized by such men as Alexander Hamilton. Then only twenty-three years old, Hamilton had already established himself as a man of brilliance and dedication. At seventeen he had written two pamphlets in answer to Tory attacks, pamphlets that displayed his fine grasp of constitutional government. He had served in the field with the Continental Army and had recently been named as Washington's secretary and confidential aide. Hamilton was convinced that the collective welfare demanded the states submit themselves to the authority of the central government.

"An uncontrollable sovereignty in each state," he told James Duane of New York, "will . . . make our nation

Alexander Hamilton.

feeble and precarious. No body but the Congress should have jurisdiction over such affairs as the making of war, peace, trade and finance."

"But the rights of the states—"

"The rights of the states must be subordinated to the rights of the Federal government for the good and welfare of all the people. The lack of a strong central government able and free to act as needed will inevitably lead to trouble. Nothing could be more injurious at home and abroad than to have a number of petty states, with the appearance only of union, jarring, jealous and perverse, without any determined direction."

Nor was he alone in fearing a federal impotency that would reduce the Congress to a debating society. George Washington grew uneasy at the lack of unanimity among Americans and issued a gloomy prediction: "I see one head gradually changing into thirteen. . . . I see the powers of Congress declining too fast for the consequence and respect which is due to them as the grand representative body of America.

Despite these, and other warnings, no changes were made. In order to enact an amendment to the Articles, unanimous approval of the states was necessary—and that seemed like a practical impossibility. Here then was the fatal flaw in the Articles of Confederation. It was a static document, unchangeable, unable to be adapted to the growing needs of the people, an instrument of government that could not endure.

By mid-1778, ten states had approved the Articles; New Jersey, Delaware, and Maryland still held out. Small states all, with precisely defined boundaries and no hope for expansion, they feared the power possibilities of their larger, richer neighbors, who made claims to the great expanses of land to the west. More and more men came to realize that a government that owned no national domain was more a league of independent states than a sovereign country.

Despite her doubts, New Jersey ratified in November and Delaware did likewise six months later. Only Maryland stood opposed, and with reason.

Virginia, large and threatening alongside, made strong claims on additional land. Were these claims fulfilled, Maryland feared Virginia would sell off the western territory and so provide herself with an immense income without being forced to tax her citizens. This would encourage people to move to Virginia in order to avoid paying taxes in Maryland. The burden on those remaining behind would inevitably be increased. In time, Maryland feared, she, and other landless states, would be left almost without population and bankrupt.

The validity of this attitude was recognized and, in the interests of unity and patriotism, states with land claims began to accede to the wishes of the landless. New York led the way in 1780, surrendering its claims in order "to accelerate the federal alliance." Later that same year, Congress took steps to resolve the dispute, urging that "the several states having claims to vast and unappropriated lands in the western country, turn over a liberal cession to the United States for the common benefit of the Union."

This drew a negative reaction in Virginia. Concessions were demanded. "Private speculators," it was claimed with some justification, "have made prior purchases of western land. These must not be recognized by the Congress, if Virginia is expected to abdicate her rights in these areas."

Another issue arose. Men like Thomas Jefferson and

Richard Henry Lee agreed that a republic could not exist if it covered more than a limited amount of territory. If spread too thin, they insisted, it would grow weak and either disintegrate into anarchy or become a monarchial despotism.

"Virginia," Jefferson said, "must voluntarily limit her size for the future welfare of the republic."

Ironically, men of the highest principles thus came to the same conclusions as those seeking only personal profit.

Then Connecticut joined New York in agreeing to surrender her land claims. Under mounting pressure, the General Assembly of Virginia altered its thinking "for the sake of the public good," and on January 2, 1781, it was agreed to cede the western claims north of the Ohio River to the United States. Specific conditions were attached that gave evidence of sincere concern with the future of the young nation.

Virginia insisted that the cession was valid only on certain conditions: that the Articles of Confederation be ratified by all the states (Maryland still had not signed); that all deeds and grants from the Indians to private parties be nullified; that certain areas be set aside as bounties for soldiers; that the lands in question be made into new states not more than 150 miles square, nor less than 100 miles square, to be admitted eventually to the union with the same "rights of sovereignty, freedom, and independence as the other States."

This voluntary limitation of size and wealth by Virginia provided an equal share of the West for all Americans. It guaranteed that those who settled there would become first-class citizens, that there never would be subordinate colonies, that the United States was not embarked on an imperialistic course.

Nevertheless, Maryland, still strongly influenced by land speculators, hesitated. Matters finally were brought to a head because of British raids in the Chesapeake Bay area. Maryland appealed to the French Ambassador to assign French naval vessels to counter these attacks. Ambassador La Luzerne overreached his authority by injecting himself into the internal affairs of the United States.

"Perhaps," he told Maryland's leaders, "the ships of the French navy will be otherwise occupied on those occasions when English privateers appear. Unless, of course, the enthusiasm of French sailors when this state ratifies the Articles of Confederation is so high that they insist on plying these waters in celebration."

The message was not lost on his listeners, and in February 1781 Maryland ratified. On March 1, the Confederation was formally announced and on the next day the first legal form of government for the United States went into effect.

During all of this, the fighting had continued. In May of 1780 (the previous year), Charleston, South Carolina, fell to the British; American losses were put at 5,000 men and 300 cannon. It was a costly blow and appeared to mark the end of South Carolina as an active participant in the rebellion. Hundreds of patriots promptly offered their pledge of loyalty to King George, and British forces occupied strong points throughout the state.

Before departing for New York, Sir Henry Clinton remarked: "If a French or Spanish fleet does not interfere I think a few works if properly reinforced, will give us all between this and Hudson's River."

About this time, rumors of peace were heard and it was said that Congress would turn over to the British the two southernmost states. Something had to be done to counter such talk, and on June 23 Congress issued a resolution which stated:

> That this Confederacy is most sacredly pledged to support the liberty and independence of every one of its members; and . . . will unremittingly persevere in their exertions . . . for the recovery and preservation of any and every part of these United States that has been or may hereafter be invaded or possessed by the common enemy.

Guerrilla warfare erupted in South Carolina and in Georgia under such daring leaders as Francis Marion, Andrew Pickens, and Thomas Sumter. Washington sent 1,400 fighting men under the command of Baron de Kalb to help. They moved against a British post at Camden, but were severely defeated by the troops of Lord Cornwallis.

Inflated by the triumph, dazzled by dreams of glory and the prospects of even greater victories, Cornwallis, never a cautious strategist, pushed his way north at the head of 8,000 troops. He failed to reckon with a hostile and armed population. Soon they began to make their anger felt, inflicting considerable damage on the British. Acting swiftly to take advantage of the developing situation, Washington ordered Nathanael Greene into the area to organize the resistance and put it to the best use.

Greene allowed Cornwallis no rest. He struck in a series of swift, damaging attacks, using surprise and mobility to counter the enemy's greater power. But Cornwallis stubbornly continued his march, advancing into Virginia. Now Greene turned his attention further to the south, making sure that no help would reach Cornwallis from that area, and causing much distress to the garrisons at Charleston and Savannah.

In Virginia, Cornwallis tried to deal with the natives, to convince them to surrender. It didn't work, although Thomas Jefferson, governor of the state, failed to get the militia to fight effectively.

The Marquis de Lafayette, come from France to help America, was at Richmond with 1,200 men; Anthony Wayne was heading for Virginia from Pennsylvania with 1,000 riflemen; and Baron von Steuben was recruiting around Charlottesville.

Cornwallis dispatched raiding parties into the countryside, but they had little success. Increasingly concerned, he ordered fortifications erected at Yorktown.

Here it was! Exactly what Washington had been waiting for. A chance for a major victory, the decisive battle. He acted quickly. Making it appear as if he intended to strike New York, feinting toward Staten Island—thus pinning Henry Clinton in place—Washington began a forced march into Virginia.

By the end of August, French Admiral de Grasse had brought his ships up from the West Indies and blockaded the James and York rivers, Cornwallis was cut off from the sea. There would be no escape by that route. And no reinforcements.

Washington arrived at Yorktown late in September to join the siege already under way. He commanded 9,000 Americans plus 7,800 French troops. Heavy cannon fire was directed at the British positions. After five days, two key posts were stormed and taken. When his efforts to retake the two posts failed, Cornwallis realized that he was

The surrender of Cornwallis at Yorktown.

finished. Defeat was only a matter of time. On October 19, he surrendered himself and his 8,000 men.

When word of Yorktown reached England, Lord North cried out: "Oh, God! It is all over!" And so it was, to all practical purposes.

Everyone but George III knew that England was beaten. No further campaigns were launched against America, though the British continued to struggle elsewhere against the Spanish and French for another year, and with some success. During that period, diplomats sailed back and forth across the English Channel with proposals and counter-proposals, terms and suggestions, questions and answers, until at last, on September 3, 1783, the final treaty was signed. America had won its freedom. With it came new responsibilities.

And new troubles.

12

After Yorktown, some people were convinced that the Revolution had achieved its purpose: the severing of all ties between the thirteen colonies and England, so that Americans could direct their own economic and political fate. But much more was involved, though its significance was lost on many of those who lived through the struggle. Men failed to understand how deeply and profoundly the Revolution would shape the future and the lives of millions of people.

There were some who saw the end product of the fighting as chaos. All institutions were effectively leveled, they claimed, and the former colonists existed now in a "state of nature." Everything, it was said—schools, laws, churches, businesses, towns, boundaries—would have to be created over again.

Those Americans were passionately patriotic. But that patriotism was more often directed to an individual than toward the federal government. Government was frequently considered a hindrance, a threat, an offensive institution, to be ignored, except when its aid was required. A man was first of all a Virginian, a New Yorker, a Georgian, a Pennsylvanian. Only after that was he an American with broad national loyalties and responsibilities. Many Americans failed to realize what it was they had accomplished— the creation of a new *nation*.

The separate states reflected the sentiments of the individuals. Each was inordinately proud of itself, its rights and privileges, and each meant to protect and propagate them, fearful that a sturdy central government might diminish its own sovereignty. Out of such attitudes, the independent states began to establish laws by which their citizens might live in peace and prosperity.

This was no new thing. The colonies had been established under written charters, had existed by their provisions for years. But now something new was required. Proper government subordinate to society. A system able to survive any change of government, no matter how radical.

Following the outbreak of fighting at Lexington and Concord, royal governors had fled America, and the provincial congresses, generally not different in composition from the old colonial assemblies, had assumed control. Then came the Continental Congress, which advised the people to establish state governments. To do so, the British constitution was used as a guideline. Admiration for traditional English law had never lessened and the people were certain that, despite the rebellion, they had remained faithful to its provisions, betrayal coming instead from King and Parliament.

"The excellence of the English constitution," colonial thinkers pointed out, "was no protection against tyranny."

"Safeguards are needed to prevent any future government from duplicating the situation."

"But how? Once authority is granted can it be abridged . . . ?"

Obviously, two kinds of government were required, local and federal. The states were successful in creating the former: ten state governments were created prior to 1776, the rest before 1780. Despite flaws, these institutions went further in the direction of individual liberty than any body of law or government then in effect.

The British constitution had been *unwritten,* based on historical precedents, easily distorted and molded to the political aims of those in power. The new states were determined to create a firm line of defense against any such inroads on their liberty.

John Adams said: "The people want a standing law to live by." Here was a desire rooted in their past.

From such political theorists as English philosopher John Locke came a remarkable and revolutionary idea—democracy based on natural law. All power, it suggested, was derived from the people. And the people were to be governed by properly appointed officials. The Americans drew on their long relationship with England for common law, keeping many of the institutions under which they had formerly lived. The result was broad similarities in the state constitutions.

Some constitutions were drafted by provincial congresses. It took the people of Massachusetts to recognize and mark this threat. In 1778, the Bay State rejected the constitution provided by their legislature, though many citizens agreed that it was ". . . a document with which a man could live."

"Still not to be accepted," others said. "People should make a constitution out of which a government may be born and exist, not the other way around."

"A government that can create a constitution can also change it and that is the road to tyranny."

Such reasoning gave birth to the idea of a constitutional convention, which was held in 1780. Out of this came a document designed by the people acting independently of government. The advantages of this system were apparent to most Americans; and, though most of the states had already made and adopted their constitutions, it was a procedure which would be followed when the time came to create a federal government.

Even though written by provincial congresses, state constitutions did assume that the people were the source of political power. Virginia, for example, asserted in its Bill of Rights that ". . . all power is vested in and consequently derived from, the people; that magistrates are their trustees and servants, and at all times amenable to them." It was a concept other states found admirable and they adopted it.

By long experience, Americans were accustomed to slicing away at the authority of the King and his representatives, the royal governors. Now, as if by reflex, they whittled away at the executive power of their own state governments. Since there was no office of hereditary right, every state officer had to be elected directly or indirectly by the people. In some cases, legislatures elected the governor and could as easily impeach him, making him subject to their desires. Pennsylvania went further—she abolished the office entirely. Governors were frequently prohibited from vetoing any legislative act and were unable to dissolve legislative meetings.

"We are plagued now," said John Adams, "by a system of weak and ineffectual executive officers, and this troubles me."

"Would you have us create other despots in the place of George III?" he was asked.

It was a question repeated by many Americans, even while others called for a strengthening of both central and state governments.

"We have no need for a powerful executive to rule over us," it was pointed out, especially by farmers and those living along the frontiers of the young country. These men, used to fending for themselves, wanted a minimum of official interference in their lives. "State assemblies represent our interests and will see to our needs."

"I fear otherwise," Adams argued. "I hold that a popularly elected governor must own a considerable amount of authority."

"In order to tyrannize us?"

"In order to protect the rights of the people from an overly ambitious legislature, to act as a check to such a body. It is all very well to view such assemblies as being concerned with the interests of the citizenry but quite a different matter to insure that end."

"What promise have we that the one will not inevitably dominate the other to the despair of us all?"

"I believe that institutions must be formed in order to best protect the interests of the people," Adams explained.

"Thus, I favor an assembly composed of two separate chambers, the approval of each necessary to make every law."

That drew strong opposition. "We need only one house, a company of ordinary citizens."

"Nonsense! What is required is a chamber composed of the best people, the best minds, those most fit to rule."

"We want no House of Lords in these United States."

"Why not both?" Adams asked reasonably. "Certainly one chamber should be composed of people from every area of the nation, every segment of society. But an upper chamber might indeed be a profitable thing. Let us provide a sanctuary for conservative men of property. Here the rich and the powerful may be contained so as not to endanger the liberties of the multitude."

"And who will see to the interests of men of property?"

Adams had the answer to that question as well. "Serving in an upper chamber, such men could act to modify any extravagant schemes put forth by the unthinking masses, and *they* could do likewise."

Adams was convinced that in America, as in every other society of men, an aristocracy would come into being. If not of birth, it would be one of station or wealth or talent. He hoped to restrain any such group. The logic of his position was such that all the states except Pennsylvania established legislatures made up of two separate chambers.

Compromise was the clay out of which the various state constitutions were sculpted, a struggle for dominance between men of substance and the poorer masses, between radical and conservative, each seeking to advance his own interests.

Each constitution generally contained a Bill of Rights which indicated precisely those liberties government could

John Adams.

in no way diminish or terminate. Freedom of the press was guaranteed, and trial by jury, the right to petition, habeas corpus and due process of law. General warrants were forbidden, as were standing armies.

There was wide variance when it came to upholding the principle that all men were born free and equal. Some Americans, it seemed, were less equal than others.

Pennsylvania's constitution was liberal, with the middle class and the frontiersmen taking political control. As a result, those living in the western portion of the state received representation equal to those in the east, something not true in all instances. In Virginia, where conservatives dominated, a middle-of-the-political-road document was produced. South Carolina was even more conservative. Here a man had to own at least fifty acres of land in order to vote, and to hold office he needed even more property. A senator had to be worth two thousand pounds, a governor ten thousand. This permitted the wealthy plantation owners along the seaboard—about twenty percent of the population—to dominate the other four-fifths of the state.

Those who owned no property, it was generally agreed, possessed little stake in the society. Said the Virginia Bill of Rights: ". . . all men having sufficient evidence of permanent common interest with, and attachment to the community, have the right of suffrage."

Nowhere in the United States did *all* adult men have the vote. And women did not have it at all. Americans were not prepared to put into effect proportional representation and universal suffrage. Equality was a convenient word. Its use provided men with a sense of righteousness, but few Americans were anxious to follow it to its logical end.

Such limitations hardly troubled most people. And with reason. Circumstances in America made certain that no great gulf existed between classes. There was, for the most part, no lofty and rich nobility and no impoverished peasantry, except for slaves. It was generally agreed that property qualifications were not going to establish an entrenched ruling clique. After all, approximately ninety percent of all Americans tilled the soil, owned their own land, had reason to believe that in time they would be able to increase their holdings.

The war itself had brought about great changes. Proprietary landholders had been deprived of their land under the Revolution, and many private estates belonging to Tories had been sectioned off and sold. This put an increasing amount of land in the hands of men who had never before owned any. Here then was a sector of the population with newly acquired property that provided them with political authority, elevated them socially, seemed to secure their economic future.

To further distribute property, inheritance laws were reformed. Before, when a man died without leaving a will all his property would pass into the hands of his oldest son, a practice called primogeniture. To insure this, there were specific laws which forbade the division of an estate. This was called entail. It was Thomas Jefferson who spearheaded the attack on these feudal customs so that by 1800 eleven of the states had decreed that all heirs must share in an inheritance. North Carolina prohibited daughters from inheriting property, if there were sons in the family; and in New Jersey, daughters received only a half-portion. Land reform guaranteed that there would be no landed aristocracy, at the same time strengthening the democratic movement.

Religion had always been in the foreground in America. Now there was a rising sentiment toward separation of church and state, the degree varying in the different states. In Massachusetts, the Congregationalist (Puritan) Church was dominant and there was conflict with other sects. The state constitution declared that people could worship when and how they pleased, though it insisted that each man must attend a place of worship on certain days. It guaranteed that no law would be passed that would subordinate one faith to another. In practice, however, matters were quite different. All communities taxed all residents for the support of local ministers, and most of that money went to Congregational parishes.

Of all the New England states, only Rhode Island practiced a high degree of religious tolerance.

In New York, freedom of worship was declared in the constitution of 1777, but with qualifications. Anyone who wanted to become a citizen had to renounce foreign allegiances, civil *and* religious. This provision effectively excluded Catholics. Clergymen were forbidden to hold office, and so were Jews, since all officeholders had to be practicing Christians.

In New Jersey, officeholders had to be Protestant. Delaware and Pennsylvania prohibited state-supported churches or restrictions on freedom of worship. Maryland allowed all men to attend the churches of their choice. North Caroline declared that no citizen should be forced to contribute to any any church and that no church should be given a preferred status. Georgia provided religious freedom for everyone; and South Carolina guaranteed civil and religious equality for all members of Protestant denominations.

In Virginia, where the Anglican Church was officially privileged, the battle for religious freedom was fierce, sparked by Jefferson, who characterized it as "the severest contest in which I have ever been engaged."

The fight was protracted, the first victory coming in 1777, when compulsory church attendance and financial support for Anglicanism were terminated. Two years later, the church establishment itself was ended. But Jefferson was defeated in his attempt to gain full religious equality and freedom. Part of the opposition came in the form of a bill offered by Patrick Henry, aimed at state support for all churches.

Jefferson persisted, and finally in 1786 his Act for establishing Religious Freedom was passed. In part, the preamble said:

> . . . that to suffer the civil magistrate to intrude his powers into the field of opinion, and to restrain the profession or propagation of principles on supposition of their ill tendency, is a dangerous fallacy, which at once destroys all religious liberty; . . . and finally that truth is great and will prevail if left to herself, that she is the proper and sufficient antagonist to error, and has nothing to fear from the conflict . . .

It was Jefferson who, with the help of his youthful followers James Madison and George Mason, would be mainly responsible later for making religious freedom a part of the federal Constitution. As a result, the United States has never suffered from religious wars or persecutions, though private intolerance has continued to exist in some people.

With all the consideration of freedom, political, religious, and economic, it was inevitable that Americans would turn an unhappy eye on the institution of slavery. There were about six hundred thousand slaves in the new nation, and men found it increasingly distasteful to declare for their own freedom while this condition existed.

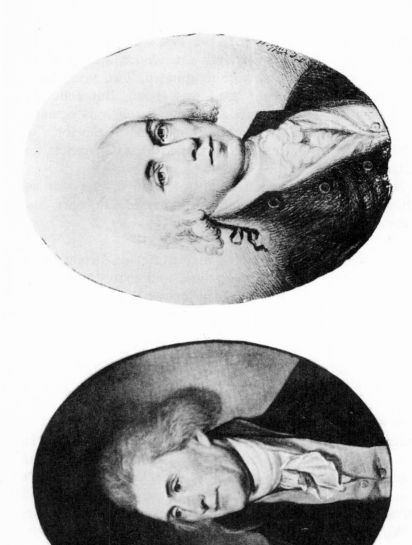

Thomas Jefferson and James Madison.

Patrick Henry said: "I believe a time will come when an opportunity will be offered to abolish this lamentable evil."

There was agitation toward this during and after the Revolution. Pennsylvania took a step in this direction by freeing children born to slaves, though they could be considered servants until their twenty-eighth year. Quakers, in order to remain in the good grace of their church, had to free all slaves. And the "Pennsylvania Society for Promoting the Abolition of Slavery, and the Relief of Free Negroes, unlawfully Held in Bondage, and for Improving the Condition of the African Race" was formed.

The Massachusetts Bill of Rights insisted that all men were born free, and the state supreme court interpreted this to mean that slaves should be given their freedom.

New Hampshire felt similarly. Rhode Island and Connecticut provided for gradual emancipation. New York formed an abolitionist society and established a school for freed slaves. Virginia made a strong effort for emancipation by passing laws that would have freed slaves; such statutes were later repealed. Maryland also had an abolitionist society. The remainder of the southern states lagged behind, doing little or nothing.

Efforts were also made to put an end to indentured white servitude. This covered large numbers of people who came from England, Ireland, Scotland, and Germany, selling themselves for a certain period of time.

Attempts were made to enact enlightened penal legislation. With Jefferson and Madison again leading the way, Virginia managed to amend existing criminal codes, ending the death penalty for all crimes except treason and murder. But progress was slow. In some states, as many as twenty offenses were punishable by death, even for a first offender. Extended sentences at hard labor, maiming, the stocks, branding, and whipping were common punishments for lesser crimes. Debt for as little as sixpence could result in a prison term of four months.

There was also an increasing concern with education. Steps were taken in various states ". . . for the more full and complete Establishment of a public School of Learning." Lands were set aside for this purpose and monies were used to establish academies. Religious groups built schools such as Erasmus Hall in Brooklyn, sponsored by the Dutch Reformed Church, and Andover and Exeter in Massachusetts.

Colleges also came into being. Medical schools in Philadelphia and New York were encouraged. The teaching of the law, however, lagged far behind, only William and Mary College dealing with this vital area. Interest in libraries was revived, and books destroyed during the war were replaced. These were mainly private institutions supported by private funds. In the matter of public education there was more talk than action. Formal education in the new nation was far from universal.

The Revolution had stretched across class lines and geographical divisions. No one person owned a monopoly on patriotism, though from time to time one group or another would seek to advance its own fortunes in the name of patriotism. Yet despite differences, three million Americans labored for a new and better country, a country like no other the world had ever seen.

13

With the Revolution ended, with the Articles of Confederation the law of the land, with the Congress the prime institution of government, the United States focused on its day-to-day existence. Many problems existed. Most of the citizens scattered throughout the thirteen states lived along the coast and were not anxious to brave the rigors of the wilderness. Travel was difficult; roads were in poor condition and coaches slow and uncertain. To journey from Boston to New York took three uncomfortable days. In the South, there were few roads, and travelers went either on horseback or by foot.

Early America was an agricultural society, people living off what they grew. Since little industry existed, they themselves made whatever was needed in the way of clothes or tools. Wind and animals, water and people supplied the power for their endeavors.

Because of the distances between towns and villages, and the difficulties of travel, each man became almost totally responsible for himself and the few neighbors he might have. State governments came to be thought of as something alien, and the Congress was looked upon as a body of men whose deliberations bore little relation to life as it was lived away from Philadelphia. No civilized nation ever had less government than did the United States, and its very nature made it less competent as time wore on. The immutable Articles of Confederation promised no help.

In the critical period after the close of the Revolution, the prospects for the new country did not appear bright. Doubts rose everywhere about her ability to solve present and future problems. European nations were hardly pleased with this experiment in liberty and self-government. It offered a living reminder to their own people that such a thing was possible, and for the most part they offered little concrete assistance.

Congress, Washington commented, was "a half-starved" creature lacking the authority to govern or to restrain the states. As if to prove him right, a band of angry veterans of the Continental Army marched on Philadelphia in the summer of 1783 to demand back pay they claimed was due them. Congress, a penniless, helpless assembly, was forced to flee to Princeton for safety.

Each day the flaws in the Articles of Confederation became glaringly more apparent. Congress could not regulate commerce, nor could it appoint or elect a national executive, a lack severely felt. No system of national courts existed. And Congress could collect no taxes; if, for any reason, funds were not forthcoming from the states, nothing could be done about it. Boundary disputes between the states existed—New Hampshire and New York both made claims to what is now Vermont; South Carolina and Georgia conflicted over the Savannah River, Virginia and Maryland over the Potomac. Congress could do nothing.

Under a weak government, men often sought to settle quarrels by themselves. The Tennessee area of North Carolina was a rugged frontier and here life was restive. Marauding Indians were a constant threat. And flatboatmen returned from marketing their goods in New Orleans complaining of the high-handed methods of Spanish officials. Efforts to get federal help were futile. Congress talked and talked—but did nothing. Thoroughly disenchanted, the settlers soon became incensed when they learned that North Carolina had ceded her western lands to the United States. A meeting was called in a log courthouse at Jonesboro, with John Sevier, soldier of the Revolution and Indian fighter, the chairman.

Those at the meeting were fiercely independent people, unruly, forced by circumstances to fend for themselves. When things were not to their liking, they acted to change them. The first speaker said it clearly.

"Don't like the whole idea of a federal government. Bad enough belonging to a state, any state. Man ought to be able to run his own affairs without interference."

Another rose. "I agree. Any government is too much government. Means taxes and laws and people coming around to say what a man's to do. Don't want none of it."

So it went, until a motion was made that the three counties represented at the meeting—Washington, Greene, and Sullivan—secede from North Carolina and form a separate state. It was a daring idea, and for a long moment there was no response. Then a great shout of approval went up. The state of Franklin had just been born.

But not even those rambunctious frontiersmen expected their state to exist without the forms of government necessary to orderly procedure. A governor was elected, John Sevier. Courts were established, laws made, taxes levied— the very conditions they had earlier decried.

People began to argue the merit of Franklin's action, some seeing it as consistent with the revolutionary spirit, others condemning it as arbitrary and subversive. Friends of long standing parted over the issue, characterizing each other as blackguards and traitors.

From the start Franklin was in trouble. Her leaders had hoped for early recognition from Congress, and when that failed to come the destiny of the new state was sealed. To further aggravate the situation, Franklin failed to live up to a treaty enacted earlier by Sevier with a group of lesser chieftains of the Cherokee tribe. According to its provisions, Franklin was to surrender the territory along the Holston River. The Indians complained to Congress about the situation and special commissioners were sent into the area to make an investigation. The commissioners signed the Treaty of Hopewell, upholding Cherokee claims.

At about this same time, many Franklinites began to grow disenchanted with John Sevier's autocratic rule. There were suggestions that a return to North Carolina might be in order. Desperate to maintain the independence of Franklin, Sevier made contact with Spanish officials, hoping to form an alliance and a treaty of commerce with their nation. It was a futile effort.

John Sevier.

North Carolina had already instituted steps designed to bring the recalcitrants back into line. First, it forgave all tax debts of men who accepted state authority. Next, it named officials to take charge of Franklin itself. Several of Sevier's slaves were seized by officers of North Carolina in return for his failure to pay taxes. This resulted in a pitched battle, a minor civil war. Sevier's forces were defeated, put to rout. Determined not to create a martyred hero, and so enlarge the trouble, official pardon was extended to Sevier. Franklin was allowed to expire with a minimum amount of attention.

There were other problems. At the close of the Revolution, trade with England had been resumed, though the English viewed the erstwhile colonies suspiciously, and with cause. Certain individual states refused to conform to the terms of the peace treaty. They continued to confiscate property which belonged to Loyalists and failed also to pay their debts.

Such leading citizens as Washington; Hamilton, then a member of the Continental Congress; James Monroe, also in Congress; John Marshall, already established in Virginia because of the brilliance of his legal arguments; and others exercised their influence to get the states, and individual Americans, to comply with the treaty terms. It did little good. The prestige of the United States diminished further.

Spain continued to be a problem. Firmly entrenched in the southwest portions of the continent, she was anxious to limit American expansion and trade opportunities in the West. To this end, Spain canceled the Right of Deposit at New Orleans, which had enabled Americans to use that port for their goods without duty or tax.

This resulted in some westerners dealing on their own with Spain. There were men who went even further, conspiring actively against the United States, their aim to place certain territories under Spanish domination. Unrest spread, and Washington wrote of this in the spring of 1785:

> The western settlers (I speak now from my own observation) stand as it were on a pivot, the touch of a feather would turn them any way.

All this contributed to the low esteem in which Congress was held. Many of its members began to lose interest and frequently failed to carry out their responsibilities. Often it was impossible to raise the necessary quorum of nine states needed to function; from October 1785 until April of the following year, official business could be conducted on only three days.

Funds were exhausted. There was no way to pay either those people who worked for the government or the soldiers, some of whom mutinied. Abroad, American representatives trying to make trade agreements were not paid; and there was open speculation about the wisdom of establishing a monarchy.

Witnessing this steady decline, Washington took a dim view of the future, and became convinced that drastic measures were called for. He said: "I do not conceive we can exist long as a nation without having lodged somewhere a power, which will pervade the whole Union in as energetic a manner as the authority of the State government extends over the several States."

During this period a system for settling the West began to evolve, the Ordinance of 1785 establishing the pattern. Provisions were made for a survey of the Federal territories in the West, which were to be fashioned into rectangular townships thirty-six miles square. Each square mile, containing six hundred and forty acres, was to be called a section, and each sold for one dollar. This meant that maps could be drawn and titles sold with greater accuracy. A key clause in the Ordinance reserved one section in each township for schools. The checkerboard design created by the Ordinance still marks much of the United States today.

Despite the Ordinance, discontent was on the rise. More and more voices called for the central government to be strengthened, demanding a system of laws by which to live, and effective implementation and enforcement of those laws.

It was James Bowdoin, governor of Massachusetts, who recommended that a national convention be held expressly for this purpose. The legislature approved and directed the Bay State delegation in Congress to summon the states together. But congressmen, fired with the concept of state sovereignty, did nothing.

Defiance of authority intensified and there was considerable violence. In New Hampshire, mobs rioted outside the legislature, demanding a more equitable distribution of property and paper money. In Rhode Island, merchants, fearful of going bankrupt because they were forced to accept payment for their goods in nearly worthless scrip, shuttered their shops.

The worst trouble erupted in Massachusetts. Here state taxes had exploded upward. Farmers were paying approximately one-third of their income to the state, and that in hard money, something they seldom acquired in substantial amounts. Then taxes were raised again. As if determined to compound matters, the legislature refused to print more paper money—a blow against inflation—and announced that it would not prevent foreclosures on the homes or farms of debtors. The already irascible farmers became angrier as financial pressures on them increased. With no prospect of relief, many of them faced the loss of their property. A town meeting was announced at Worcester to consider the situation, but nothing was decided. However, a week later a convention of delegates from fifty towns in Hampshire County met at Hatfield. They too made their sentiments clear to anyone who would listen.

"This body should condemn the selfishness of the state legislature. And let's put an end to lawyers practicing their wiles against those of us in cruel debt."

"The courts must cease arbitrary foreclosure. There must be tax relief for the poor citizens of the commonwealth."

Samuel Ely, once a clergyman and now a leader of the farmers, took the floor. "We must throw up our constitution . . . the constitution is broke already, the Governor has too much salary, the Judges of the Superior Court have too much salary, we can get men that will ride the circuit for half the money . . . the General Court should not sit, we will pay no more respect to them than to puppies."

More complaints were voiced. Congested court dockets meant delays in justice, and the farmers wanted that situation rectified. Again they insisted that paper money be issued so as to ease their economic burdens.

The Hatfield convention urged that changes be made by legal means. A futile desire. The temper of the farmers was such that mob action became inevitable. Courts were disrupted in Worcester, Concord, Northampton, Great Barrington, and elsewhere. Out of the turmoil, insurgent leaders appeared, articulate and angry men. There were Job Shattuck and Luke Day, and Daniel Shays, a captain during the Revolution and currently a bankrupt farmer.

Concerned that the farmers might unseat the state supreme court in session at Springfield, Governor Bowdoin ordered General William Shepard to that town with six hundred militiamen. When he arrived, Shepard was confronted by Daniel Shays at the head of five hundred armed and determined farmers. The militia was faced down and the court forced to disband.

This strained Governor Bowdoin's patience. He refused to be intimidated. He declared Shays and his followers to be outlaws and rebels. The legislature made matters worse. It suspended the writ of habeas corpus and passed a bill stating that any man who attended a "riotous" assembly would forfeit his ". . . lands, tenements, goods and chattels . . . (and) be whipped thirty-nine stripes on the naked back, at the public whipping-post, and suffer imprisonment for a term not exceeding twelve months nor less than six months; and once every three months during the said imprisonment receive the same number of stripes on the naked back, at the public whipping-post."

Having been given the name of rebel, the farmers decided to act accordingly. They would fight for what they wanted, and they took the view that their actions were an extension of the Revolution. However, they gained little official support. Congress authorized a force to be raised in New England, ostensibly to fight Indians but actually aimed at putting down this rebellion.

Job Shattuck led an unruly mob at Concord, men mostly drunk and disorderly. When some Massachusetts militia units appeared, the farmers broke and ran, Shattuck among them. He was trapped in the woods near Groton, wounded

Shays' Rebellion.

when he put up a fight, and captured. His followers scattered.

Meanwhile, Shays made plans. He had raised a force of twelve hundred farmers, plus Luke Day's men, and with them intended to attack the federal arsenal at Springfield. To counter this, Governor Bowdoin raised some fifty thousand dollars. The money came from wealthy businessmen who understood that if this rebellion were not suppressed they might lose everything they owned. The money helped recruit an army of about four thousand volunteers, under General Benjamin Lincoln.

The attack was scheduled for January 1787. But on the appointed day, Luke Day failed to materialize with his men. Undaunted, Shays launched his attack at the arsenal, which was protected by General Shepard and his troops. Shepard had hoped to avoid bloodshed, but it was impossible. The rebels advanced determinedly until they were only a few hundred yards from the arsenal itself. Inside were stored 450 tons of equipment and munitions, 7,000 muskets, 1,300 barrels of gunpowder, considerable shot and shell, bayonets, swords. Possession of these arms would turn any mob into a well-equipped and dangerous army.

Shepard called upon Shays to halt. The farmers kept coming. Shepard ordered a cannon volley fired over their heads. The warning failed to slow the advancing men. Having run out of choices, Shepard commanded his men to shoot to kill. When the smoke cleared, four rebels lay on the ground, three dead, one dying. The others ran.

The next day General Lincoln arrived to deliver further punishment to Shays and his men. At the beginning of March, the farmers were routed at Petersham, and Shays fled to Vermont. He was later pardoned, officials convinced that the rebellion had been motivated by honest desires for economic and social reform.

Shays' Rebellion had positive results. The Massachusetts legislature subsequently passed laws lowering court costs and exempting personal property and tools of trade from seizure for debt. It also opposed an increase in direct taxes.

The significance of the rebellion was felt everywhere in the United States. It had dramatically underscored the great gulf between the "haves" and the "have-nots." George Washington, conservative in outlook and not given to wild fancies, commented on the degenerating situation in the country: "There are combustibles in every state which a spark might set fire to. I feel infinitely more than I can express for the disorders which have arisen. Good God! Who besides a Tory could have foreseen, or a Briton have predicted them?"

Thomas Jefferson, then in Europe, listened to much criticism of the unruliness in his homeland. He pointed out that there was considerably more disorder in the kingdom of France than in republican America. In a letter to James Madison, he said: "I hold it, that a little rebellion, now and then, is a good thing, and as necessary in the political world as storms in the physical."

Though chaos and trouble thrived under the Articles of Confederation, there was also some good. To encourage settlement in the lands now belonging to the United States north of the Ohio River and east of the Mississippi, Congress enacted the Ordinance of 1787. This provided a government for the region. Congress would appoint a governor, a secretary, and three judges. When five thousand free males resided in the territory, a legislature was to be convened, and when the population reached sixty thousand, a constitution could be written and application for statehood made. Eventually from three to five states were to be made up out of the region. When admitted to the Union, the new states were to be equal in every way to the original thirteen. Freedom of worship and trial by jury were guaranteed to all people, and it was provided that no man born in the territory should be a slave.

This Northwest Ordinance, as it came to be known, was the most important achievement of the Congress under the Articles of Confederation. It signaled the start of the great western migration by Americans and also strengthened federal authority. Once again it was made clear that the young nation had no interest in creating colonies. Instead people were encouraged to practice self-government and move toward eventual statehood.

Despite the benefits of the Northwest Ordinance, it was increasingly evident that only limited progress could be made under the Articles, though that attitude was expressed by a comparatively few men. Fear of centralized power was still strong. People spied tyranny in any official act that might limit their activities.

Matters were coming to a head. And responsible men were worried. They remembered Shays' Rebellion, the state of Franklin, the trouble in the Southwest. And remembering, they grew more firmly convinced that the time to rectify the swiftly disintegrating situation was at hand. Constructive action had to be taken to keep the nation from tumbling into a sump of despair and conflict.

And it was.

14

Virginia and Maryland had been at odds with each other for a long time. Tax money was the root of the problem. The Maryland charter of 1632 had located the southern boundary of that colony along the southern bank of the Potomac River, and permitted her to regulate and tax the boats of those Virginians shipping cargoes on the river. To complicate matters, the mouth of the Chesapeake River fell within Virginia's territory. Tolls were levied on Maryland's ships to help defray the costs of beacons and the lighthouse in the channel. These tolls and taxes created hostile feelings among the citizens of the two states, and efforts to resolve their differences had come to naught. But in 1784, James Madison, after three years in Congress, and now head of the Virginia Assembly Committee on Commerce, decided to do something. He called for a conference, to be held in Alexandria.

After the Revolution, George Washington had retired to his home at Mount Vernon and announced that he was finished with public life. Now he let it be known to Madison, and the other delegates to the conference, that he was deeply interested in its deliberations. And with cause. As were most planters at this time, Washington was in debt, with obligations he was anxious to meet. Outside of Mount Vernon, his only other business was the Potomac Company, of which he was president. The company aimed to make travel on the river cheaper and easier so that vessels could more readily reach the western lands, some of which were owned by its shareholders. Navigation had to be facilitated if the company was to expand its operations.

But the Alexandria meeting accomplished nothing. The delegates were without specific instructions and not truly prepared to negotiate. It was about to dissolve itself when Washington spoke.

"Gentlemen," he said. "This dispute, which we all of us hope to terminate in a matter favorable to both sides would best be served under more agreeable circumstances. My home at Mount Vernon is open to you all and there in comfort this business might find itself more readily resolved for my house is indeed a well resorted tavern."

The delegates adjourned happily to the big house on the banks of the Potomac, where, with Samuel Chase of Maryland and George Mason of Virginia chairing the proceedings, they continued their deliberations. Out of this came a statement favoring uniform taxes in order to

George Washington and his family bid farewell to General Lafayette at Mount Vernon.

secure the prosperity of both states, interstate cooperation in defense as well as commerce, and annual meetings aimed at advancing the welfare of the two states.

Here was progress—but not enough to satisfy James Madison. He recognized that the federal government alone could truly regulate trade, domestic and foreign. Having considered the problem at length, he drafted a resolution in January 1786, to which the Virginia Assembly readily agreed, inviting all the states to convene in order ". . . to take into consideration the trade of the United States . . . to take into consideration the relative situations and trade of the said States."

Response was less than enthusiastic. Five states sent a total of twelve commissioners. Four others appointed delegations which were delayed en route. The remaining four ignored the matter entirely. Conspicuous among those missing was Maryland.

The convention took place at Annapolis in mid-September, the delegates instructed to discuss interstate commerce and the broader aspects of developing trade in America. The only ones with authority to even consider "other important matters" were the New Jersey representatives.

Alexander Hamilton, representing New York, took the floor to say it was apparent to him that this sparsely attended meeting could not speak for all the states. All attention riveted on him as he spoke. Owning an already impressive reputation, Hamilton was cool and authoritative, dashing and handsome, with a colorful and varied history. Born in the West Indies, he had been educated at King's College (now Columbia University) in New York. He was a confidant of George Washington, a soldier, a member of

Congress, a lawyer, somehow more aristocratic than those who claimed that status by birth.

"Gentlemen," he began, "to talk of trade between this state and that state is fitting but not sufficient to the situation. I hold that the problems facing the nation are greater and require serious deliberation before we are reduced to anarchy and confusion."

"What do you suggest, sir?"

"I have taken the liberty of preparing a letter to the Congress emphasizing the grave condition the country finds itself in, demanding that steps be taken to strengthen the Articles under which we all exist . . ."

Hamilton was a man accustomed to leading, to giving orders, and many men were offended by this attitude. In the end, James Madison of Virginia, slight and wizened, was able to bridge the gap. He softened the tone of the letter, *asking* where Hamilton had *demanded*. Finally the instructions which had been issued to the New Jersey delegation became the basis for a summons to a nationwide meeting on the second Monday in May, to be held in Philadelphia, a meeting that would: . . . "devises such further provisions as shall appear . . . necessary to render the constitution of the Federal Government adequate to the exigencies of the Union . . ."

On that note, the Annapolis Convention was adjourned and the delegates returned to their homes. Alexander Hamilton was convinced a pressing need existed for a strong central government. He was certain the nation could not survive for very long in the face of disorders such as Shays' Rebellion. His arguments were well known: The United States had to be fashioned on a firm and powerful base, and that meant a sound currency, established public credit.

It meant also a government able to conduct foreign affairs with authority and dispatch. It meant the maintenance of armed forces and all the other necessary departments and organs of a stable government. The Articles of Confederation made no provision for these, and Hamilton was convinced that unless something were done soon disaster would result.

But these views were not unanimous. There were men of comparable stature in Congress who supported the Articles, men who feared federal authority. As a result, four long months passed before agreement was reached in Congress that a convention of the thirteen states was ". . . expedient . . . for the sole purpose of revising the Articles of Confederation and reporting to Congress and the several legislatures such alterations and provisions therein."

Washington didn't want to attend. There were affairs that required his personal attention. His mother and sister were ill, and his rheumatism seemed to be getting worse. There was another reason. The prospects for success at Philadelphia were dim, and to attend a convention that failed would only damage his prestige. But Madison and Virginia's Governor John Randolph kept insisting that it was his duty to participate. In the end they prevailed. Washington consented to go to Philadelphia.

In May, the weather went bad. Heavy rains turned the roads into strands of mud, delaying the arrival of many delegates. But come they did and finally, on May 25, with rain falling steadily, the convention got under way at the old Pennsylvania State House (later called Independence Hall) on Chestnut Street. On that first day, only twenty-seven delegates were present, but before the convention ended there would be a total of fifty-five. Benjamin Franklin

Early Independence Hall.

was the oldest of them at eighty-one, and Jonathan Dayton of New Jersey at twenty-six was the youngest.

Some men were conspicuous by their absence. Samuel Adams, for one, and Patrick Henry, who claimed he "smelled a rat" in the assemblage. Thomas Jefferson and John Adams were in Europe. Rhode Island was the only state that did not participate.

The delegates settled into their chairs, side by side in curving rows facing the speaker's platform at the east side of the spacious chamber with its tall windows, all of them aware that this was where the Declaration of Independence had been signed.

The first order of business was to choose a president. Robert Morris rose to speak and a hush filled the hall. There was little doubt as to what he would say. He nominated George Washington. Edward Rutledge seconded immediately. Without discussion, a vote was taken. Washington was unanimously elected. Morris and Rutledge escorted him to his place behind the desk on which the Declaration of Independence had been signed, and he settled into the high-backed speaker's chair with its gilded and carved sun, which seemed to be either setting or rising—it was not clear which.

His blue eyes grave, Washington gazed out at the delegates, some of whom had never seen him before. He was a big man with a thick, strong body and sloping shoulders, large of hand and foot. His ruddy complexion and tranquil expression gave him the look of a practiced outdoorsman, a horseman, which he was.

He began to speak haltingly, his words not always clear, for his false teeth, made of wood, fitted badly. But this was of no consequence. Here was a man used to command, one whom other men had gladly followed and would again. He thanked the delegates for the honor bestowed on him. He reminded them that he was without experience in such a role but would do his best, hoping his errors would be understood and excused. Gouverneur Morris later quoted him as saying:

It is too probable that no plan we propose will be adopted. Perhaps another dreadful conflict is to be sustained. If to please the people, we offer what we ourselves disapprove, how can we afterwards defend our work? Let us raise a standard to which the wise and honest can repair. The event is in the hand of God.

Almost from the beginning, the leaders among the delegates disregarded their states' instructions to do nothing but amend the Articles of Confederation. These men were convinced that the fate of the Union was at stake and drastic action was in order. Many among them recalled vividly the words Dr. Benjamin Rush, one of the delegates, had spoken the previous January.

There is nothing more common than to confound the terms of the American revolution with those of the late American war. The American war is over: but this is far from being the case with the American revolution. On the contrary, nothing but the first act of the great drama is closed. It remains yet to establish and perfect our new forms of government; and to prepare the principles, morals, and manners of our citizens, for these forms of government, after they are established and brought to perfection.

Out of such sentiments came the conviction that an entirely new form of government was required. It was a startling idea, frightening, and the convention decided to meet behind locked doors, to keep their deliberations secret. The official journal was published in 1819, and the private records of some delegates eventually were made public.

In the debates that followed, when differences ignited tempers and threatened to end the convention before something productive had been accomplished, there was always at least one delegate to remind his fellows of the reason they had assembled, of the need for their deliberations to continue.

Once it was Gunning Bedford of Delaware, himself a strong supporter of the principle of states' rights. "The condition of the United States," he told his listeners, "requires that something should be immediately done."

And on another occasion it was Elbridge Gerry of Massachusetts: "The fate of the Union will be decided by the convention."

And Caleb Strong, also of the Bay State: "It is agreed on all hands that Congress are nearly at an end. If no Accomodation takes place, the Union itself must soon be dissolved."

Such thoughts were enough to blur the differences among them. Each delegate began to consider mutual interests rather than those of his own state. None of them wanted to contemplate the chaos that would result if the government were to fall.

Such a disaster would have brought rejoicing in England, then holding hard to posts in the Northwest, and waiting for calamity to befall the former colonies. And, to the Southwest, Spain continued to maneuver overtly and covertly, her intention to weaken further the already unsteady federal apparatus. This, and the recurrent domestic outbreaks of violence, foretold worse times in the future, if nothing were done. It was a desperate situation.

Now prepared to begin its business, the convention gave its attention to Edmund Randolph, governor of Virginia, on May 29. It was rumored that Randolph harbored some radical plan, and the delegates strained to hear his words. Randolph's proposals would alter the original course of the convention, and become the basis for the federal Constitution. They came to be known as the Virginia Plan.

He began by enumerating the flaws in the Articles of Confederation, building a case for what was yet to come. "Under the Confederation this nation is helpless to stand against any foreign invader for it has no power to raise an adequate army. Nor can it prevent or punish treaty infractions by the several states. Nor protect those states, nor raise monies as are necessary."

He continued to review the situation, concluding his litany of weakness and failure by bluntly stating that the Articles required total revision so that they might promote ". . . the common defense, security of liberty and general welfare of the nation. To accomplish this, the central government must be strengthened and made national in character."

Alert to the sensitivity of some of his listeners who had signed the Articles of Confederation—John Dickinson, Robert Morris, Gouverneur Morris, and Elbridge Gerry— Randolph was careful not to ascribe any defects to its authors. He characterized them as patriots, wise men but limited because of ". . . the then infancy of the science of constitutions, & of confederacies."

He presented the Virginia Plan, in the main the work of James Madison's fine mind, explaining each of its fifteen resolutions. The plan called for a two-chambered congress, members of the lower house to be elected by the voters, members of the upper house nominated by the state legislatures. Congress would have the power to tax, to control commerce, to make war and peace. It would also choose a supreme court and lower courts. More, it would name a chief executive. In him would be vested those powers heretofore enjoyed by the Congress under the Articles. The executive, and certain federal judges, would act as a council of revision with a veto power over the legislature.

The next day, Charley Pinckney of South Carolina introduced a plan for a ". . . draught of a federal government to be agreed upon between the free and independent States of America."

This caused Alexander Hamilton to speak for the first time, and there could be no doubt about his meaning. He wanted to know if the United States were to be a loose and impotent collection of states of varying sizes and powers. Or would it become a single national government?

The question concerned Charles Pinckney. He wondered if Randolph meant to abolish state governments entirely.

"Not at all," was the reply. "Each state will surrender only those powers which are specifically granted under the Plan to the federal authority."

Gouverneur Morris rose to speak: "I say we do not yet have any sort or kind of federal government, for such a government has a right to compel every part to do its duty. The federal government and the state governments cannot both be supreme. Either there is one government, or none. We had better take a supreme government now, than a despot twenty years hence—for come he must in the resulting anarchy that must ensue without central authority."

George Mason spoke of laws that would ". . . directly

operate on individuals, and would punish those only whose guilt required it, to distinguish between men . . ."

The debate continued. Each resolution was discussed and argued, altered to suit the temper of the convention. Words became issues. The phrase "too republican" was replaced with "too democratic" and men said "nation" when they meant "federation." In time, the terminology became more precise; and, what is more important, the delegates eventually drew together in outlook and sentiment.

They began to understand that it was possible to form a federation of states, each of which would have authority in *local* matters, at the same time conceding to a central government the power to legislate, to judge and administer those questions which affected *all* the states. This was to be a government created out of the consent of the people, their elected delegates making laws and enforcing them.

George Mason said: "We ought to attend to the rights of every class of the people."

It was an idea radical enough to make certain members of the company uneasy.

15

The work went forward. It was decided that a national legislature would have to be superior to those of the states. Pinckney objected. He wanted to specify what state laws should be deemed improper and therefore valid for the attention of the national legislature. Others, including Madison, spoke against such limitations.

Eventually, the debate turned back to a chief executive. For some of the delegates, that meant a king. For others a plural executive made sense. And what powers would he (or they) possess? How long would the term of office be? How was the executive to be selected? And what about payment, salary, expenses?

Benjamin Franklin opposed paying a salary to the executive. He wrote, and his words were read to the convention: "Sir, there are two passions which have a powerful influence on the affairs of men. They are ambition and avarice; the love of power, and the love of money. Separately each of these has a great force in prompting men to action; but when united in view of the same object, they have in many minds the most violent effects."

Washington, however, favored a powerful executive, expressing his position later in a letter to his wartime comrade, Lafayette:

> There cannot, in my judgment be the least danger that the President will by any practicable intrigue ever be able to continue himself one moment in office, much less perpetuate himself in it . . . Though, when a people shall have become incapable of governing themselves and fit for a master, it is of little consequence from what quarter he comes.

How to select a chief executive? Should Congress elect him? The idea troubled the delegates, for it would inevitably make him subservient to that body. On the other hand, a popular election excited much adverse criticism.

Said Roger Sherman: "The people are not sufficiently informed for the responsibility."

And George Mason: "One might as well refer a trial of colors to a blind man."

Finally a compromise was made, through the efforts of Gouverneur Morris and James Madison. It was based on the method Maryland used in choosing its state senators— a body of electors. Each state was to have a number of electors "equal to the whole number of Senators and Representatives to which the State may be entitled in the Congress" and this "electoral college" would vote for a single executive, to serve a four-year term.

Here was an idea that drew approval even from such a conservative as Alexander Hamilton, who had hoped that a lifetime executive might be appointed with the power to name state governors. Still, he agreed with this latest concept, saying he was certain that "it would prevent any cabal, intrigue, and corruption."

So in the end it was a single executive, an executive with veto power over legislation, though any vetoed bill might subsequently be passed "by two thirds parts of each branch of the national legislature."

Differences of opinion continued to divide the delegates. Much of it was focused on the question of how the members of Congress were to be elected. The smaller states were against representatives being chosen on the basis of population, for fear that their voices would become subordinate to the larger states. This resulted in the New Jersey Plan, which sought to protect the states with fewer people. It called for a single executive body with a single vote for every state, a plural executive with a diminished authority, and a supreme court.

William Paterson of New Jersey, after detailing the differences between his plan and Virginia's, said: "Our object is not such a government as may be best in itself, but such a one as our constituents have authorized us to prepare, and as they will approve."

In effect this was a claim that the Virginia Plan could not be ratified, that the convention was empowered only to revitalize the Articles of Confederation, not to form a new federal government. They were alarmingly close to losing all they had worked for.

Edmund Randolph took the floor in defense of the plan he had offered. He emphasized that the time cried out for severe measures, that the precise source of their authority to act was less important than the need to do so, that this might indeed be the last chance for the new nation to turn away from a calamitous future.

"When the salvation of the Republic is at stake," he said, "it would be treason to our trust not to propose what we find necessary." Should they fail, he went on, "the people will yield to despair."

The argument intensified; federal rights, states' rights, individual rights. James Wilson, a nearsighted Scotsman from Pennsylvania, asked with passion, "Can we forget for whom we are forming a Government?" He challenged, "Is it for *men,* or for the imaginary beings called *States?* Will our honest constituents be satisfied with metaphysical distinctions? Will they, ought they to, be satisfied with being told that one-third compose the greater number of States? The rule of suffrage ought on every principle to be the same in the second as in the first branch. If the Government be not laid on this foundation it can be neither solid nor lasting. . . .

"Bad governments are of two sorts,—first, that which does too little; secondly, that which does too much; that which fails through weakness, and that which destroys through oppression. Under which of these evils do the United States at present groan? Under the weakness and inefficiency of its government. To remedy this weakness we have been sent to this Convention. If . . . we shall leave the United States fettered precisely as heretofore; with the additional mortification of seeing the good purposes of the fair representation of the people in the first branch, defeated in the second."

Benjamin Franklin.

Others spoke, taking one side or the other, and finally Dr. Franklin heaved himself erect, this time to speak for himself.

"The diversity of opinions turns on two points. If a proportional representation takes place, the small States contend that their liberties will be in danger. If an equality of votes is to be put in its place, the large States say their money will be in danger. When a board table is to be made, and the edges of planks do not fit, the artist takes a little from both, and makes a good joint. In like manner, here, both sides must part from some of their demands. . . ."

Franklin offered a compromise motion that was promptly attacked by both sides. Gunning Bedford of Delaware stated the cause of the small-state men in a loud and angry voice: "I do not trust you, gentlemen. The large States dare not dissolve the Confederation. If they do, the small ones will find some foreign ally, of more honor and good faith, who will take them by the hand and do them justice."

Rufus King of Massachusetts voiced his shock at Bedford's words: "I am grieved that such a thought entered his heart. I am more grieved that such an expression dropped from his lips. The gentleman can only excuse himself on the score of passion. For myself, whatever might be my distress, I would never court relief from a foreign power."

So it went, until Roger Sherman of Connecticut came up with an acceptable compromise. He suggested that members of the lower house of the new Congress be elected according to population; and each state have one vote in the upper chamber. Though subsequently modified, this plan provided the foundation for the House of Representatives and the Senate as they are today.

The delegates moved ahead. They provided for a supreme court, and lower courts.

And the convention gave Congress the right "to regulate Commerce with Foreign Nations, and among the several States, and with Indian Tribes . . . [but] the Migration or Importation of such Persons as any of the States now existing shall think proper to admit, shall not be prohibited by the Congress prior to the year one thousand eight hundred and eight."

This last referred of course to slaves. At the same time, the authority to collect a tax of no more than ten dollars for every Negro brought into the United States was given to Congress.

And taxation. Here too slavery was a question, as it continued to play a role in every facet of national life. The South wanted its large Negro population exempted from direct taxation. The North insisted that, if slaves were to be counted when it came to representation, it was equitable that they also be counted when it came to levying taxes. Views were exchanged until it was finally decided that "Representative and direct Taxes shall be apportioned among the several States . . . according to their respective Numbers, which shall be determined by adding to the whole number of free Persons . . . three fifths of all other Persons."

In writing what was to become the Constitution, the delegates in Philadelphia's State House had to work out the specific powers belonging to the federal government, as well as those to be retained by the states. This resulted in a duality of government, the concept of union coexisting with the state. But neither at the mercy of the other. The Founding Fathers labored to effect a balance, to develop guidelines for a middle course, not at all certain which direction the new "federalism" would eventually take.

Nevertheless, there were those who stood opposed to the Constitution as it took shape, arguing that another convention should be called for at a later date. It was never held.

Perhaps none of the delegates was wholly satisfied with what resulted from their deliberations. But in fact more had been accomplished than they realized. They had replaced the Articles of Confederation and its many weaknesses with a form of government of infinite political strength and resiliency. A union had been forged in which sovereignty actually resided with individuals, not state or local governments. Further, under this new Constitution both federal and state governments would take their strength from a single source—the authority of the people, who were citizens not only of their particular states but of the nation at large. The Constitution extended federal authority to the most remote and isolated corners of the nation; and, for the first time, it became possible for individuals to influence issues that were national.

The delegates possessed no illusions that ratification by the states would come easily. They anticipated loud and stormy objections to those portions of the Constitution which reduced the power of particular groups or special interests, or which inhibited the ambitions of various states or sections.

"But the decision must rest with the people," it was generally agreed, "whether to reject or approve this document."

To allow this to happen, it was necessary to bypass state governments, to seek approval, after transmission to Congress, from specially elected conventions in each of the states. In this way, the voice of the people should be heard.

In order to prevent one or two dissident states from frustrating the will of the majority, it was decided that approval by nine states would be sufficient to make the Constitution into the law of the land.

Finally accepted by the delegates in State House, the Constitution was ready to be signed. The clerk read its provisions, and when he was done it was old Dr. Franklin who called for unanimity.

He was to be disappointed. Three delegates—Edmund Randolph, Elbridge Gerry, and George Mason—refused to sign. Thirty-nine men did endorse the Constitution. For various reasons, the remainder were absent.

The members moved forward to put their names on the Constitution. Dr. Franklin watched benignly, gazing at the gilded sun carved on the presiding officer's chair. He turned to the delegates around him and murmured: "I have often and often, in the course of the Session, and the vicissitudes of my hopes and fears as to its issue, looked at that behind the President without being able to tell whether it was rising or setting: But now at length I have the happiness to know that it is a rising and not a setting Sun."

That same afternoon, William Jackson, secretary to the convention, busied himself destroying all the various papers and notes left in his charge. He was scheduled to depart for New York City the next morning, carrying to the Congress, there in session, the signed Constitution.

That evening, George Washington, alone in his rooms, made the following entry in his diary:

Monday, 17th. Met in Convention, when the Constitution received the unanimous vote of 11 States and

Colonel Hamilton's from New York (the only delegate from thence in Convention), and was subscribed to by every member present except Governor Randolph and Colonel Mason from Virginia and Mr. Gerry from Massachusetts.

The business being thus closed, the Members adjourned to the City Tavern, dined together and took a cordial leave of each other; after which I returned to my lodgings, did some business with, and received the papers from the Secretary of the Convention, and retired to meditate on the momentous work which had been executed, after not less than five, for a large part of the time Six, and sometimes 7 hours sitting every day, except Sundays and the ten days adjournment to give a committee opportunity and time to arrange the business, for more than four months.

If General Washington felt that the war was won, he was mistaken: only the first battle had been fought.

"We the people of the United States, in Order to form a more perfect Union, establish Justice, insure domestic Tranquility, provide for the common defence, promote the general Welfare, and secure the Blessings of Liberty to ourselves and our Posterity, do ordain and establish this Constitution for the United States of America."

"We the people of the United States . . ." The words seemed to express everything the Revolution had been fought to achieve. But not all men thought so, and opposition sprang up throughout the nation.

First, in the Congress. The Constitution was considered by that body on September 26. Richard Henry Lee, of Virginia, on whose resolution the Declaration of Independence was based, took sharp exception to it. He was convinced that it did not go far enough in the cause of liberty and justice.

"This document," he told all who would listen, "must contain a bill of rights specifically *guaranteeing* the freedom of all men, and it should contain too a provision establishing a council of sorts to advise and assist the President. Moreover, I would have it make common law and trial by jury secure everywhere in these United States so that men might find justice under the law. And I am for eliminating the office of the Vice-President."

As the argument intensified in Congress, Lee offered a list of amendments which he felt should be added before the Constitution was submitted to the states. In this he found himself in the minority and assailed those who opposed him.

"They are attempting," he cried, "to push the business on with dispatch . . . that it may be adopted before it has stood the test of reflection and due examination."

Despite his efforts, it was agreed that the Constitution would receive no congressional recommendation, but would be "submitted to a convention of Delegates chosen in each state by the people. . . ."

By stagecoach and by boat, copies of the Constitution went out to each of the states. Locally, it was published in newspapers and printed in pamphlet form, reaching almost all the people, being read aloud to those who couldn't read. Its adherents worked hard to see that it reached everyone, firm in the belief that its provisions would cause support to swing to it.

Advocates of ratification became known as Federalists, and included Washington, Hamilton, Franklin, and Madison. Much of their support came from the wealthy and educated segments of the country, lawyers and businessmen, speculators and merchants, shippers and plantation owners. These people were convinced that only a strong central government could end the internal squabblings that threatened the public welfare and also protect American interests abroad. Even the most fervent supporters of the Constitution admitted its shortcomings, but they were not deterred.

"It is a finer structure on which to build a nation," they claimed, "than the Articles of Confederation."

The Anti-Federalists were equally dedicated to their cause, equally enterprising in advancing it. George Mason published his objections in a newspaper, the *Pennsylvania Packet,* and forwarded a copy to Washington. Edmund Randolph gave the Virginia House of Delegates his reasons for not signing the Constitution, insisting that a second convention was required. Elbridge Gerry notified the Massachusetts legislature of his sentiments, and Richard Henry Lee sought ways and means of postponing ratification. He wrote to Randolph, making the letter public:

. . . adopt it: if wrong, amend it at all events: for to say, as many do, that a bad government must be established, for fear of anarchy, is really saying, that we must kill ourselves, for fear of dying.

The Anti-Federalists insisted that the United States was too large to be governed by a single central administration, that such an administration would become dictatorial if allowed the authority necessary to rule effectively. They feared the large states would dominate the smaller ones, that the President might become another kind of monarch. There were other objections to the Constitution: Congress would become too much like Parliament; a sound fiscal system would do irreparable harm to debtors; the limitations of the document meant the Revolution had been fought in vain; and, again and again, that it contained no Bill of Rights.

Cautious men and fearful men made common cause in the name of Anti-Federalism. An office-seeking politician in North Carolina's back country told his listeners that a federal capital would inevitably be a walled city with a huge and powerful army poised to reduce the liberties of the people. In Massachusetts, a farmer named Amos Singletary was also against ratification: "These lawyers," he said, "and men of learning, and moneyed men, that talk so finely, and gloss over matters so smoothly, to make us poor illiterate people swallow down the pill, expect to get into Congress themselves; they expect to be the managers of this Constitution, and get all the power and all the money into their own hands, and then they will swallow up all us little folks."

Among the Anti-Federalists were such ardent revolutionists as Patrick Henry and Samuel Adams. Adams wrote:

> . . . I stumble at the threshold. I meet with a national government, instead of a federal union of sovereign states . . . If the several states in the union are to become one entire nation, under one legislature, the powers of which shall extend to every subject of legislation, and its laws be supreme and control the whole, the idea of sovereignty in these states must be lost.

An angry Patrick Henry asked: "What right had they to say, *we the people?* My political curiosity, exclusive of my anxious solicitude for the public welfare, leads me to ask, who authorized them to speak the language of, *we the people,* instead of *we the states? States* are the characteristics and the soul of a *confederation.* If the states be not the agents of the compact, it must be one *great, consolidated, national government of the people of all the states."*

And Richard Henry Lee insisted again that the powers of the central government were not clearly defined in the Constitution, that popular liberties were not suitably protected.

In Philadelphia, an Anti-Federalist who called himself "Centinel" published his views, insisting that it was the wealthy who coveted power and sought ratification:

> . . . These characters flatter themselves that they have lulled all distrust and jealousy of their new plan, by gaining the concurrence of the two men [Washington and Franklin] in whom America has the highest confidence, and now triumphantly exult in the completion of their long meditated schemes of power and aggrandizement. I would be very far from insinuating that the two illustrious personages alluded to, have not the welfare of their country at heart; but that the unsuspecting goodness and zeal of the one has been imposed upon, in a subject of which he must be necessarily inexperienced, from his other arduous engagements; and that the weakness and indecision attendant on old age, has been practiced on the other.

No one could miss the point: "Centinel" thought Washington was incapable of making a reasoned and intelligent decision and he considered Dr. Franklin to be senile. Others disagreed.

Alexander Hamilton began to publish a series of letters explaining the Federalist position in the *Independent Journal* in New York, signing them "Publius." He enlisted James Madison and John Jay in writing as well, and eventually their essays—eighty-five in all—were collected and published in a book, under the title *The Federalist,* which Jefferson termed "the best commentary on the principles of government ever written."

One of the most sensitive areas under debate was the question of separation of governmental powers. Said Hamilton:

> . . . it is evident that each department . . . should be so constituted that the members of each should have as little agency as possible in the appointment of the others . . . all the appointments for the supreme executive, legislative, and judiciary magistracies should be drawn from the same fountain of authority, the people . . .

In Pennsylvania, as elsewhere, passions flared hotly over the issue. There was some violence, and abuse was directed at both sides. James Wilson tried to explain the Federalist position to a crowd in front of the State House.

"Understand," he cried, "that every power not specifically alloted to the Federal government in the Constitution is retained by the States. Thus the States are not destroyed but own a new strength instead. I say it is those officials who fear they may find themselves without those positions of considerable comfort and less work who fear the Constitution, afraid that . . ."

An Anti-Federalist broke in: "Believe nothing James Wilson tells you! He is one of the principal fabricators of that dark conclave that made this Constitution . . ."

John Jay.

When the state constitutional convention gathered, the debate followed more orthodox lines. Wilson addressed them in these words: "America has it in her power to adopt either of the following modes of government: She may dissolve the individual sovereignty of the States, and become one consolidate empire: she may be divided into thirteen separate, independent and unconnected commonwealths; she may be erected into two or more confederacies; or, lastly, she may become one comprehensive Federal Republic."

Thomas McKean, chief justice of Pennsylvania, spoke for adoption, ending: "I move, gentlemen, that this convention ratify the proposed Constitution at this time."

John Smilie of Fayette County rose to object. "Justice McKean and his cronies are attempting to rush the deliberations of this body, to hurry us without due time to consideration, to stampede us into adopting."

There were denials and further accusations, and the debate continued. William Findley, of Westmoreland County, claimed the Constitution would establish "a consolidated government, and not a confederation of the states. It is a compact between individuals entering into society, and not between separate states enjoying independent power, and delegating a portion of that power for their common benefit . . . from the very nature of things, a state can have only one voice . . . but there cannot exist two independent sovereign taxing powers in the same community, and the stronger will of course annihilate the weaker . . . the new government must surely eradicate the states."

Wilson responded. "The secret is now disclosed and it is discovered to be a dread that the boasted state sovereignties will . . . be disrobed of part of their power . . . Upon what principle is it contended that the sovereign power resides in the state governments? . . . My position is, that the sovereignty resides in the people. They have not parted with it; they have only dispensed such portions of it as were conceived primarily for the public welfare . . . the people are the source of authority . . . they may take from the subordinate governments powers with which they have hitherto entrusted them, and place those powers in the general government . . . gentlemen will please to remember, this constitution was not framed merely for the States; it was framed for the PEOPLE also."

Benjamin Rush, an ardent Federalist, raised his voice. "I would be happy to see Pennsylvania surrender sovereignty to the United States. I have now a vote for Members of Congress. I am a Citizen of every State."

"Nonsense," Smilie cried. "No matter what changes are made in the Confederation, the rights of mankind must be remembered."

Partisan sentiments aside, George Washington viewed the debate as an indication of national character, saying:

> . . . . a greater Drama is now acting in this Theatre than has heretofore been brought on the American stage, or any other in the World. We exhibit at present the Novel and astonishing Spectacle of a whole People deliberating calmly on what form of government will be most conducive to their happiness; and deciding with an unexpected degree of unanimity in favour of a System which they conceive calculated to answer the purpose.

On December 7, news reached Pennsylvania that Delaware had ratified. John Smilie said gloomily: "Delaware has reaped the honor of having first surrendered the liberties of the people."

Five days later, Pennsylvania ratified, the vote 46 to

23. New Jersey was next, then came Georgia, Connecticut, Massachusetts, Maryland, South Carolina, and New Hampshire, the ninth state to ratify. Virginia and New York were the sites of prolonged and bitter argument, both eventually ratifying by close votes. In November 1789, with the Constitution already in operation, North Carolina ratified; and Rhode Island, after considerable urging from the other states, did likewise in 1790.

The struggle for ratification was an exercise in fundamental Americanism, the right of dissent in practice, the various sides of a political question being aired publicly and for the most part peacefully. The stakes were high and men believed deeply. Out of the debate, and the Federalist and Anti-Federalist camps, there would come into being political organizations, which with time and circumstance would alter and modify themselves, always struggling to shape the direction of government in a way that best suited themselves. So it may be said that the Constitution actually gave birth to the two-party system in this country.

More important, the Constitution signaled the appearance of a new kind of government. Here was an instrument for expressing the identity of the people as a nation, for extending the dreams and ambitions for which the Revolution had been fought. Americans had suffered to protect their property, to insure their liberty, to withstand the inroads of tyranny; the Constitution was designed to aid them in this continuing struggle.

The men who helped create the Constitution, those who hammered out its provisions, those who wrote it, and those who stood for it, knew that with ratification they were moving into a new arena. The Constitution was a foundation on which to construct the future, a living monument to them all.

17

"Our Constitution is in actual operation; everything appears to promise it will last." The words were Dr. Franklin's; he concluded on a note of caution. "But in this world nothing is certain but death and taxes."

The first Congress under the new Constitution convened April 1, 1789. Anxious to get on to the business of tabulating the electoral votes so as to be able to announce the name of the first President of the United States, the Senate decided not to wait for a quorum. On April 6, with both the Senate and House of Representatives in joint session, it was announced, to no one's surprise, that George Washington had been elected President. John Adams, with the next highest vote, was named Vice-President.

It was a week before the news reached Washington at Mount Vernon and he made ready to assume this newest duty and honor. His diary on April 16 included these words:

> About 10 o'clock I bade farewell to Mount Vernon, to private life, and to domestic felicity; and with a mind oppressed with more anxious and painful sensations than I have words to express, set out for New York.

It was a triumphant journey. In Alexandria and Baltimore he was hailed by friends. Philadelphia feasted him publicly and he was cheered in Trenton. At Princeton, the president and faculty of the college welcomed him warmly, pledging their support. Thirteen pilots in white uniforms ferried him across the Hudson River on a specially built barge and thousands of people cheered from gaily bedecked craft in the harbor. At last he set foot in New York, the temporary national capital, to the salutations of ceremonial cannon. It was April 23.

One week later, at noon, Washington was escorted to Federal Hall. There he was led into the Senate chamber and formally presented to the members of Congress.

This done, John Adams indicated that it was time for the oath of office to be administered. The President-elect nodded gravely and walked out onto the balcony.

The streets below were crowded with cheering people. They called out encouragement and good wishes to the Virginian. He presented an image of solidity and sobriety, a big man in dark brown homespun, white stockings, and buckled shoes, solemn and strong. A plain military sword hung at his side. He was almost sixty years old, but he carried himself with dignity, head high, shoulders back.

It was Robert R. Livingston, chancellor of the State of New York, who administered the oath. The ceremony concluded, Livingston swung back to the people below and cried out: "Long live George Washington, President of the United States!"

With the sound of the people still echoing, Washington stepped back inside and in a voice barely audible delivered his inaugural speech to the Congress. He proposed no particular program. Nor did he issue a clarion call to action. Instead, typically, he asked his listeners to put private interests aside and consider the public good and the future of the whole nation. He finished with a prayer:

> Almighty God, we make our earnest prayer that Thou wilt keep the United States in Thy holy protection; that Thou wilt incline the hearts of the citizens to cultivate a spirit of subordination and obedience to government; to entertain a brotherly affection and love for one another and for their fellow citizens of the United States at large.

It was widely held that no man was more ideally suited to be President than Washington. He was a commanding figure who seemed to own all the qualities of leadership in proper proportions. Jefferson described his character as being "in its mass perfect, in nothing bad, in few points indifferent; and it may be truly said, that never did nature and fortune combine more perfectly to make a man great."

A symbol Washington was, but the times demanded more. Unlike the men who subsequently held the office of President, he did not inherit an already functioning governmental structure. Almost an entire government had to be created and set in motion. Everything had to be considered, everything had to be done. Even the Congress had to order itself, establish rules by which to function, discover the most efficient manner of operation.

Among the first items of business for Congress was to write and submit to the states a Bill of Rights, safeguards of individual liberties. Demanded by five of the states when the Constitution was ratified, this had been pledged by Federalist spokesmen.

James Madison introduced in Congress the Bill of Rights, twelve amendments to the Constitution. Two of them, one dealing with salaries for congressmen and the other concerned with the makeup of that body, were never passed. The remaining ten were approved by the states and proclaimed in 1791.

The Bill of Rights inhibited the central government, preventing it from becoming too powerful. The First Amendment reads:

> Congress shall make no law respecting an establishment of religion, or prohibiting the free exercise thereof; or abridging the freedom of speech, or of the press; or the right of the people peaceably to assemble, and to petition the Government for a redress of grievances.

The next nine amendments are concerned with the establishment of a regulated militia, a prohibition against quartering soldiers in peacetime without consent, no unreasonable search or seizure, and judicial rights such as the guarantee of a swift and public trial, the right of counsel, the right not to testify against one's self, a prohibition against cruel and unusual punishment, no excessive bail, and more. The Bill of Rights concluded with Article Ten:

The powers not delegated to the United States by the Constitution, nor prohibited by it to the States, are reserved to the States respectively, or to the people.

In accord with the Constitution, the Supreme Court, as well as lower courts, was established. John Jay was the first Chief Justice of the high court and Edmund Randolph the first Attorney General. Other departments came into being. Jefferson was named Secretary of State; Henry Knox of Massachusetts, Secretary of War; Samuel Osgood, Postmaster General; Alexander Hamilton, Secretary of the Treasury. Washington made a practice of meeting with these four men, seeking their advice on various governmental matters. This informal council eventually became the presidential Cabinet, as it is known today.

Money matters were a prime concern for the young government. From its inception, the country was faced with a debt of about eighty million dollars, foreign, domestic, and state included. Daily expenses added to this. Something had to be done, and Alexander Hamilton acted accordingly.

He advanced a series of far-reaching economic proposals. He suggested that the federal government assume the total national debt, including the obligations of the states. To earn money to pay this, and so elevate the nation's foreign credit, he advocated the sale of new securities.

Hamilton got what he wanted by promising to support a Potomac River site for the proposed national capital. In return, he was to receive the help of Madison and Jefferson in passing his economic reforms.

Next, Hamilton recommended that a Bank of the United States be established. Despite widespread opposition, the bank was established. As a result, trade and commerce increased and industry prospered, with an inevitable rise in governmental revenues.

Hamilton was not yet finished. His *Report on Manufactures* (1791) asked for a protective tariff to encourage America's "infant industries." He advocated that a mint be created so the government could coin money. The first mint was at Philadelphia; and the monetary system of pennies, nickels, dimes, quarters, half-dollars, and dollars instituted then is still in force today.

Every move Hamilton made was received with skepticism in certain quarters; and frequently his actions were denounced as unconstitutional. It was Fisher Ames, of Massachusetts, who placed matters in some perspective: "I scarce know a point which has not produced this cry, not excepting a motion for adjournment. The fishery bill was unconstitutional; it was unconstitutional to receive plans of finance from the Secretary: to give bounties; to make the militia worth having; order is unconstitutional; credit is tenfold worse."

Conflicting ideologies in the nation were becoming more pronounced and appeared to be best represented in the persons of Hamilton and Jefferson. The former, bright, youthful and ambitious, energetically plunged into one controversy after another, appearing to some to be grasping for more and more governmental power. Jefferson was different. He owned little taste for public conflict. Big and ungainly, shy, he was dedicated to the cause of the ordinary citizen, to freedom and equality of opportunity.

The opposing political forces lined up behind these two men. And it was out of this conflict, these differing philosophies on how to run the country, that political parties eventually came into being, the Federalists and Anti-Federalists, later called Democratic-Republicans.

Regional differences were making themselves felt as the end of Washington's term came near. Concerned about the lack of unanimity in the country, Jefferson, and others, urged the President to stand for re-election, aware of his reluctance to do so.

"North and South will hang together," Jefferson said persuasively, "if they have you to hang on."

Washington agreed. He again was elected unanimously. The emphasis of government veered now in the direction of foreign affairs. During this initial generation of American government, the world was rocked by more strife, more war, more revolution than it would see again until the outbreak of the First World War in 1914.

The American Revolution had a particularly powerful impact on the people of France, where poverty and injustice were the rule. Shortly after Washington took office, rebellion erupted in that country. American interest in French affairs was great, and both apprehension and approval were voiced.

The French Revolution was aimed at evils more pronounced than those that existed in America, and so gave birth to greater excesses. The French deposed their King and executed him, and a bloody terror was unloosed on the country. Soon France was involved in war with Spain, Holland, and England.

The spread of the conflict to include the English meant that the fighting would spill over into the Western Hemisphere, into the nearby Caribbean. It was feared that American shipping might be affected. Even more, the United

States and France were bound to aid each other by the Treaty of 1788. France wanted that help.

But there was no enthusiasm for war in the government. All the members of the Cabinet wanted to remain neutral and so did the President. Even Jefferson, who characterized those nations aligned against France as "Conspirators against human liberty," was afraid of what might result should the United States intervene.

On April 22, 1793, Washington issued his Proclamation of Neutrality, which would become a guideline for American foreign policy for more than a hundred years, suggesting a "friendly and impartial" course for the nation.

America's relations with England continued to be uncertain. There were still English soldiers stationed at fur-trading posts around the Great Lakes; the Newfoundland fishing banks were prohibited to Americans; and trade with the West Indies was restricted. Even more bothersome, American ships were frequently apprehended at sea by British men-of-war, and Yankee seamen were impressed into the English Navy. Further, the boundary between Maine and Canada had yet to be firmly fixed. For their part, the English were no happier than the Americans, claiming the United States had failed to fulfill its obligations to restore Loyalist property confiscated during the Revolution.

Something had to be done to ease these tensions. There was more trade with England than with any other country and to lose that source of income would have been a terrible blow. Washington acted. He sent John Jay to London with orders to negotiate a treaty. Jay succeeded in getting England to relinquish her hold on the forts in the Northwest Territory, and to permit trade with the West Indies on a limited basis. But no mention was made of impressment or fishing rights.

Meanwhile, domestic difficulties continued. Hamilton, anxious to pay off the state debts which the government had assumed, advocated an excise tax on such homemade products as distilled liquor. An unanticipated storm resulted.

Trouble began late in the summer of 1794, in Monongahela County, Pennsylvania, south of Pittsburgh. Here, whisky was more than a pleasurable brew: it was a "money crop," and a medium of exchange for the farmers, who seldom got their hands on any hard currency. In this rugged country life was difficult and not very rewarding. Whisky took the place of a balanced diet and a warm house. Those farmers could find no logic in having to pay a tax on grain which they drank instead of eating.

Popular resentment intensified until a United States marshal was shot at. Passions rose and crowds collected. Soon there was rioting. With the situation getting worse, Washington became convinced that here was a clear and present danger to the Government. He ordered ten thousand militiamen into the area. The Whisky Rebellion was put down.

During this same period relations with Spain were delicate. Free use of the Mississippi River and New Orleans was in dispute; and the border between the United States and Spanish Florida remained open to question.

Hoping to end those disagreements, Washington dispatched Charles Pinckney, then Minister to England, to Madrid. His mild but firm manner impressed the Spanish, and his efforts resulted in the Treaty of Lorenzo, or Pinckney's Treaty, in 1795. The agreement provided for navigation rights on the Mississippi, for the right of deposit at New Orleans, and established the thirty-first parallel of latitude as the southern boundary of the United States.

This treaty, and the one with the British, went a long

way toward attaining full security for the young republic. Now the prospects for extending the Union into the western territories were considerably brighter.

As the year 1796 came around, Washington found his thoughts turning more and more to home, to Mount Vernon. He was sixty-four, and considered himself to be an old man. He had had enough of public life, and wanted to return to his beloved Potomac River, to step back from the partisanship of politics, a condition which deeply distressed him. He wrote to Jefferson, no longer the Secretary of State: "I was no party man myself and the first wish of my heart was, if parties did exist, to reconcile them."

A sensitive man, Washington was also deeply disturbed by the rising tide of criticism now being leveled against his administration, and against him personally. He said to Jefferson that he had been attacked "in such exaggerated and indecent terms as could scarcely be applied to a Nero, a notorious defaulter, or even a common pickpocket."

Washington decided to retire at the end of his second term. He unearthed an address prepared for him by James Madison some years before, when he had considered retirement after a single term in office. Currently on less intimate terms with Madison, he asked Hamilton to draft a fresh version along the same lines. This was done, and then Washington went over Hamilton's words, reworking portions to his own taste, restoring a number of Madison's phrases and ideas.

It was a speech never given. Instead, Washington's Farewell Address was printed in the *American Daily Advertizer* of Philadelphia on September 19, 1796. He urged that a genuine nation be formed, warning of sectional conflicts. He voiced his fear of partisan politics which might interfere with his concept of regular governmental procedures. He indicated that he did not place much value on the efforts of voluntary organizations in the area of political education, nor was he able to perceive that a political opposition in a democracy exercised a legitimate and constructive function. He tended to identify with the Federalists, and they tended to identify government with themselves, as if they possessed some innate qualifications which made them more fit to govern than other people. He viewed opposition to those in power as divisive, if not totally subversive.

Nevertheless, it was the noble farewell of a sincere man who had served his country long and competently and wished her well. He closed with these words:

"I anticipate with pleasing expectations that retreat in which I promise myself to realize, without alloy, the sweet enjoyment of partaking, in the midst of my fellow-citizens, the benign influence of good laws under a free government —the ever favorite object of my heart and the happy reward, as I trust, of our mutual cares, labors, and dangers."

George Washington, first President of the United States, the only one ever elected without opposition. His retirement marked the end of an era. He left behind a nation obstreperous, unsettled, still seeking its own identity, facing years of strife and uncertainty, of hardship and struggle. The United States of America.

18

From a loose assemblage of thirteen colonies, to a nation—a unique experience, the first time a nation had actually been *created*. Others had come into being slowly, gradually, over extended periods, the result of their historical experiences.

Never before had colonies sundered the ties with the mother country in order to establish their own identity. This identity went further than the shape of the land: it grew out of a people of common language and interests, common hopes for the future.

But in America, life was in a state of flux. Traditions

were changing and new ones taking hold. The territory was expanding. The people, coming from various places, brought with them different customs and ways of thinking. Yet all of them eventually would become part of the American scene.

It was evident that the Declaration of Independence, the Revolution, the Constitution were only the start. The latter, for example, provided a legal framework, a form at once solid and flexible, able to accommodate itself to the needs of the people as they were transformed by time and progress.

Here, for the first time in history, a nation had come into being that derived its powers from the people, power coming from below rather than above, as had been traditional. This was no mere theory stated and quickly forgotten. A device existed for insuring this upward flow of power—the constitutional convention. The people elected delegates who drew up a constitution, which was to be the law of the land. Then it was submitted back to them for their approval. Here was the practical application of the theory that men create a government, that authority stems from the people—the rebellion legalized and structured.

It was an idea that fired the imaginations of men everywhere and it spread—the French employed it, and so did the various nations of South America. It was understood that if properly used this method would eliminate the need for violent changes in government.

As to the question of attaining a maximum of individual liberty while still maintaining law and order—this was done by fixing the limits of government. The Founding Fathers understood that no government could be allowed to wield unlimited power. This resulted in a government of laws, and one bound by the law. To guarantee this, checks and balances—the three branches of the government: executive, legislative, judicial, each able to inhibit the others—were instituted.

Because of their own unhappy colonial experience, Americans were careful not to repeat it as they expanded westward. New lands were called territories, and their inhabitants were citizens of the nation. Under prescribed conditions the territories could become states, with all the rights and privileges of the original thirteen.

The problem of Federalism, long held to be insoluble, was solved by granting dual citizenship. People automatically owned citizenship in both their states and the nation as a whole. The national government possessed those powers held to be of a general kind, while the states maintained authority in matters of a local nature. State and nation, each supreme in its own area. When conflict arose, as it inevitably did, the courts existed to pass on the questions.

Religious freedom came into being to a degree never before known. This was a necessity born of the many different faiths of the people. It was made clear that church and state were to be kept separate.

Equality under the law was enunciated. That the proposition might too often have failed in practice has resulted in Americans insisting that its application be broadened. Attempts to fulfill the claim of the Declaration of Independence that "all men are created equal" have been made —the Civil War was one—and continue to be made.

The Constitution provided for a political democracy. It made no stipulation as to from what segment of society the officers of the nation could come. The President might be rich or poor, of one religion or another, and the same held true for the members of Congress and the Supreme Court. Suffrage, severely limited in the beginning, was extended so that very few adult Americans are today excluded from exercising their right of ballot.

The American struggle for freedom encouraged men around the world in their own fight for independence. The United States was a promise fulfilled and oppressed people everywhere moved to end tyranny. No nation was immune from the hope raised by the American Revolution, by the Declaration of Independence, by the Constitution. What began at Lexington and Concord fired imaginations, and men dreamed of bettering their lives, and those of their families, their countries. Many have done so.

And the end is not yet.

Bibliography

Alden, John Richard, *The American Revolution.* Harper &
Row, New York, 1954.

Ambler, Charles H., *George Washington and the West.*
University of North Carolina Press, Chapel Hill, 1936.

Angle, Paul M., *By These Words.* Rand McNally & Co.,
Chicago, 1954.

Barck, Oscar Theodore, Jr., and Lefler, Hugh Talmadge,
Colonial America. The Macmillan Company, New York,
1958.

Becker, Carl L., *The Declaration of Independence.* Har-
court, Brace, New York, 1922.

210

Bowers, Claude G., *Jefferson and Hamilton.* Houghton Mifflin, Boston, 1925.

Chidsey, Donald Barr, *The Siege of Boston.* Crown Publishers, New York, 1966.

————, *Birth of the Constitution.* Crown Publishers, New York, 1964.

Chinard, Gilbert, *Thomas Jefferson,* University of Michigan Press, Ann Arbor, 1929.

Chute, William J. (ed.), *The American Scene.* Bantam Books, New York, 1964.

Gipson, L. H., *The Coming of the Revolution.* Harper & Row, New York, 1954.

Hanlin, Oscar, *The Americans.* Little, Brown & Co., Boston, 1963.

Hansen, Marcus Lee, *The Atlantic Migration.* Harvard University Press, Cambridge, 1940.

Jensen, Merrill, *The Articles of Confederation.* University of Wisconsin Press, Madison, 1959.

————, *The New Nation.* Alfred A. Knopf, New York, 1950.

Lancaster, Bruce, and Plumb, J. H., *The American Heritage Book of the Revolution.* Dell Publishing Company, New York, 1958.

Lengyel, Cornel, *Four Days in July.* Doubleday & Co., Garden City, 1958.

Malone, Dumas, and Rauch, Basil, *Empire for Liberty.* Appleton-Century-Crofts, New York, 1960.

Miers, Earl Schenck, *The American Story.* Channel Press, Great Neck, 1956.

Miller, J. C., *Sam Adams: Pioneer in Propaganda.* Little, Brown, Boston, 1951.

————, *The Federalist Era.* Harper & Bros., New York, 1960.

Morgan, Edmund S., *The Birth of the Republic*. University of Chicago Press, Chicago, 1956.

Morison, Samuel Eliot, *Builders of the Bay Colony*. Houghton Mifflin, Boston, 1930.

Nevins, Allan, and Commager, Henry Steele, *A Pocket History of the United States*. Washington Square Press, New York, 1942.

Schlesinger, Arthur M., *Prelude to Independence*. Alfred A. Knopf, New York, 1958.

Starkey, Marion L., *Land Where Our Fathers Died*. Doubleday & Co., Garden City, 1962.

Trevelyan, George Otto, *The American Revolution*. David McKay Co., New York, 1964.

Van Doren, Carl, *The Great Rehearsal*. Viking Press, New York, 1948.

Ward, Christopher, *The War of the Revolution*. The Macmillan Company, New York, 1952.

Index